"Here is a book that addresses having a successful life that is practical and spiritual instead of being abstract. It is a must read for any person who wants to align their life with God's purpose. Derric does a wonderful job making this subject accessible to the reader. Well done!"

—Michael C. Hyter
President and CEO, Novations Group, Inc.
Boston, MA

"This is a must read for inspiration and motivation. It will definitely bless you as you press forward to live a successful life."

—Rev. Dr. Larry E. Covington
Sr. Pastor, Ebenezer United Church of Christ
Burlington, North Carolina

"*Life in the Key of G* clearly defines for individuals practical life principles... *Life in the Key of G* is not about Gregory but about God, who has gifted Gregory with the creative abilities to make this resource available and attainable for all in their spiritual development. This book is multifaceted; it speaks to those in corporate and Christian arenas. This book is not just for the sanctified but for those who desire to be spiritually guided in an unsanctified world. Within the pages of *Life in the Key of G*, you find a gem that personifies who God is and what God can do..."

—Fredrick Amos Davis M. Div.
Pastor, First Calvary Baptist Church
Durham, NC

"I am often asked the question about balance from persons of various walks of life. D. A. Gregory's *Life in the Key of G* provides as comprehensive a perspective on a balanced life as one can get. Writing from the well of experience in both the corporate and the clergy world, he offers words of wisdom from which any person serious about effective and efficient living can benefit. Reading this book will attune you to the key of G."

—Bishop Claude R. Alexander, Jr.
Senior Pastor, University Park Baptist Church
Charlotte, NC

Life IN THE Key OF G
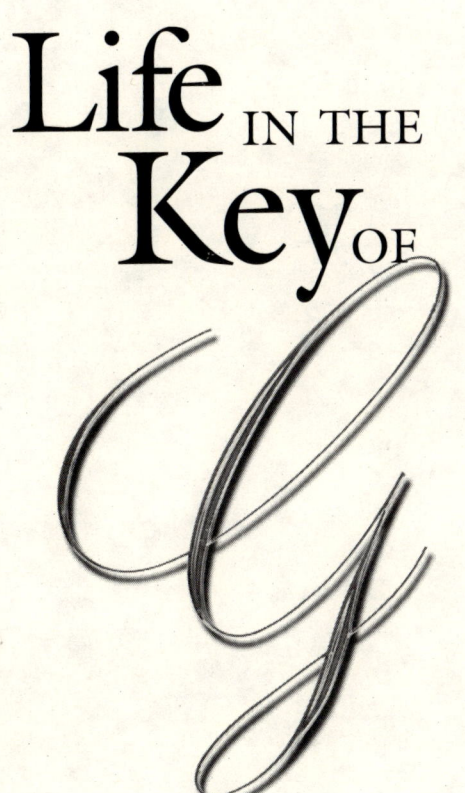

Eight Keys to Achieving Good Success

Life IN THE Key OF

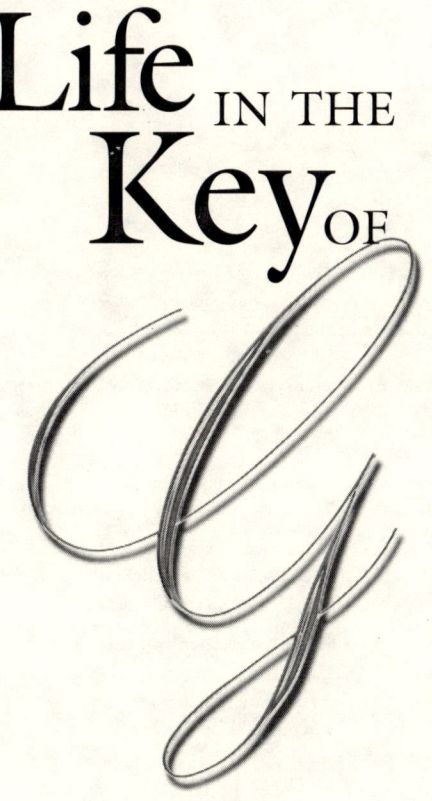

D. A. GREGORY, SR.

Tate Publishing & *Enterprises*

Life in the Key of G
Copyright © 2009 by D. A. Gregory, Sr. All rights reserved.

No part of this publication may be reproduced, stored in a retrieval system or transmitted in any way by any means, electronic, mechanical, photocopy, recording or otherwise without the prior permission of the author except as provided by USA copyright law.

All Scripture quotations are taken from the New King James Version. Copyright © 1996 by Broadman & Holman Publishers. Used by permission. All rights reserved.

Scripture quotations marked "NIV" are taken from the *Holy Bible, New International Version* ®, Copyright © 1973, 1978, 1984 by International Bible Society. Used by permission of Zondervan Publishing House. All rights reserved.

The opinions expressed by the author are not necessarily those of Tate Publishing, LLC.

Published by Tate Publishing & Enterprises, LLC
127 E. Trade Center Terrace | Mustang, Oklahoma 73064 USA
1.888.361.9473 | www.tatepublishing.com

Tate Publishing is committed to excellence in the publishing industry. The company reflects the philosophy established by the founders, based on Psalm 68:11,
"The Lord gave the word and great was the company of those who published it."

Book design copyright © 2009 by Tate Publishing, LLC. All rights reserved.
Cover design by Amber Lee
Interior design by Kellie Southerland

Published in the United States of America
ISBN: 978-1-60799-444-2
1. Religion, Christian Life, Inspirational
09.03.02

THIS BOOK IS DEDICATED TO:

Diamond, my one and only "Punkin"
Devon, the tower of power and knight in shining armor
Derric, Jr., the official "mini-me" and prince of the castle
Gabrielle, resident cheerleader clone,
princess, and baby girl
Morgan, the big baby, cheerleader, future
Academy Award winner, and drama queen
Brittany, the number one, brat, and
superstar-businesswoman-to-be
Corey, our resident big boy and
Lynnette, my fitness fanatic, friend, lover, and
companion in this adventure called life.

Acknowledgments

Without God and his love, his son, Jesus, and his sacrifice, and the abiding presence of the Holy Spirit, this book never would have been possible. God also provided special blessings in the form of special people who, along this journey, invested in my spiritual development, character refinement, and timely encouragement.

- To my mother, Sybil Gregory, who inspired me to want to know Jesus for real and for being my friend.

- To my father, Kenneth Gregory, who loved me and showed me how to be a man who did not get thin when things got thick.

- To Jane B. Erwin, the greatest mother in love on earth, and to my sisters, Ruby, Claudia, and Stephanie.

- To my brother, Kenneth, my #1, and my sister, Yvette, who has such a vibrant spirit.

- To Aunts Vivian and Uncle John, who have had my back from birth, and to the host of aunts, uncles, cousins, nieces, nephews, extended family, and frat who truly love me.

- To St. Matthew's United Methodist Church, who laid the foundation for my character and integrity.

- To Godmother Geneva Graves for taking me to Sunday school every Sunday and for Godmother Catherine Edwards for her prayers behind the scenes.

- To the Jones family "up on the mountain" in Baltimore, who paid their paperboy in pork chops and fried chicken.

- To Fred Moon and Walter Palmer, who continue to "love at all times as only real friends do."

- To Dr. Keith Reed and Pastor G. Sylvester Gaines who made the Bible practical and helped me to embrace Christian manhood as an attainable goal.

- To Wendell Shockley, James Ezell, Bishop S. Todd Townsend, and all of Sharon Baptist Church and its Mighty Men for pushing me out into the deep.

- To Pastor Fredrick Davis and my First Calvary Baptist church family for loving my family.

- To Darryl Beasley and Eddie White for going with me to Women's Empowerment when the book was still just a dream and then challenging me to make it a reality.

- To Pastor Wesley Elam and Pastor Larry Covington for being mentors, encouragers, and true friends and for creating opportunities for me to use my gift.

- To Pastor D. Z. Cofield of Houston, Texas, who validated me as a preacher.

- To: Grandma and Pop-Pop, Grandpa John and Grandma Belle, Daddy Albert and Jeral, Auntie and Ikey, Aunt Essie, Aunt Rachel and Uncle Vertis, Aunt Sylvia and Aunt Mary, Aunt Shirley, Uncle Will and Aunt Elaine, Aunt Maude, Aunt Jeanette, Uncle Milton and Aunt Jean, Uncle James, Jack and Olivia, James Earnest, DeChelle, Shelly, Eric, Jordan and Maya, Evan, Jasmine, Michael and Benjamin, Francois and Pierre, Lauren and Braxton, Cara and Sierra, all my cousins and family on this side of the Jordan, Mt. Pilgrim, and all my other church families, all my friends who know they are family, Aggie Nation "Aggie Pride," Omegas round the world, and to every reader of this book—much love!

Family matters.
Love you all and God bless you.

Table of Contents

15	Foreword
19	Introduction
21	Vertical Integration
23	Focus
29	Faith
37	Fellowship
47	Horizontal Orientation
49	Family
65	Friends
73	Resource Utilization
75	Finances
89	Follow-Through
103	Divine Participation
105	Favor
119	Epilogue
121	Unlock Your Life
123	About the Author

Foreword

What is the measure of a life? How many times have you asked this question of others? How many times have you asked for candor and sincere introspection from them, only to be confused on the topic inside your own mind? There are various standards that have been used over time to define the "value" of one's life. One standard has been to define someone by their "trappings of wealth," including appreciable assets like property, jewelry, and artwork, along with depreciable assets like cars, clothes, and furniture. Another standard of valuation is to measure someone by their net worth—in cash, stocks, and bonds or the revenue and savings they generate for their companies. Some measure it by the people they know—their influence, status, and celebrity are what give them value. But at the end of the day, what is it that will be the lasting legacy of a life—long past when the trappings lose their usefulness and the people are gone?

Derric A. Gregory is a man, friend, colleague, and peer who had all of these things as a senior African-American executive in corporate America. As a member of the Executive Leadership Council, the premier networking organization for senior African-American executives in the world, I have seen him interact with the entire gamut, from CEOs to young professionals, without fault or uneasiness. But for Derric, the access, the trinkets mean nothing without something more. For Derric, the measure of his life is centered in his deep, abiding faith, love, and commitment to his God, his family, and his purpose in life.

This became very evident at a recent meeting when Camilla McGhee, Director of Member Services at the Council, asked him to pray, having heard he was a minister. His prayer riveted the audience with its power and practicality. The buzz in the room was palpable! Something was different and distinct about the lifestyle of the person providing these words of comfort and clarity. Our members now look forward to his invocations to hear what creative story he will use to raise our spiritual consciousness. The same effect was noted when he participated on a high-profile panel for our Mid-level Managers Symposium in October 2006. Despite the fact that he was in the midst of some personal challenges in his private life, he felt his personal testimony was important to share with others. He attended and served as a panelist for the Personal Power and Leadership workshop on work/life balance and challenged the audience to make an introspective assessment about their core values. He stated, "Whatever you make the core of your life defines the context and the content of your life." We knew then that something greater than corporate fame and acclaim was central to this brother's life. He was already living his *life in the key of G* (God)!

For too many of us, we live our lives playing a character rather than fully owning how and what serve as priorities in our lives and what gives our lives meaning and value. We let other people and forces dictate our lives instead of actively living our lives through a combination of spirit, service, and sacrifice.

This book represents a life plan for those who feel they are not leading or living a full life. It's a plan whose foundation is built upon the importance of spirit, service, and sacrifice. The eight precepts in this book represent a roadmap for those who want to make their current setbacks serve as the catalyst for taking their lives to the next level. While this book has spirituality as its base, its concepts and action steps are easily convertible to the business arena from which Derric is a star participant.

So, the next time you are asked what is the measure of a life, let this book's message and action plan help you in providing the answer that works best for you. This book should motivate you to demand better of yourself and for yourself. Give yourself the right and permission to let your personal value and your life be measured by more than just the color of your credit card; let it be measured by the content of your character!

—Carl Brooks,
President and CEO
The Executive Leadership Council

Introduction

Throughout my childhood, and even as an adult, I have always loved to go to the amusement park. Whether it was Gwynn Oak Park, Kings Dominion, Great Adventures as a child or Disney World, and Busch Gardens with my children, the amusement park was big fun. There were rides, all types of kiddy rides, and the slower, pedestrian rides like the merry-go-round. You know, the merry-go-round. It goes a little up and a little down and round and round with little challenge and little change. Then, there was the roller coaster!

You know, the roller coaster; its slow ascent to its lofty heights only to get to the top, briefly pause and drop you, loop you, right side up, upside down, twists and turns, hair flying, white-knuckles fear, and exhilaration alternating with each breathtaking thrill—whew!

Life is like an amusement park. It offers different options and opportunities. Some choose the merry-go-round version; others choose the roller coaster. Neither choice is right or wrong, but if I had to choose, I'd choose the roller coaster. The exhilaration, the uncertainty, the anticipation, the rush of adrenaline from the fear, and the sweet sigh of relief when it comes to an end, quickly followed by the desire to do it all over again—that's the roller coaster, and that's life!

Don't get me wrong; there are times we all would prefer a more docile merry-go-round experience. The truth of the matter is that real life is not that way. We would love for everything to just work out when, in fact, the Apostle Paul tells us that all things *work together* for good (Romans 8:28, NKJV). There is no easy button to hit, but instead it is the combination of the up and downs, the swerves and curves, the thrills and chills that work together to make life worth living.

Life in the Key of G is written to those who desire to successfully manage their way through the ride of life. The book offers eight key elements segregated into four major themes of vertical integration, horizontal orientation, resource utilization, and divine participation, addressing fundamental relationships and activities that are critical components of this adventurous ride called life.

So, strap in, buckle up, and enjoy the reading and the ride!

Vertical Integration

Focus

"Whatever you determine to be the core in your life will define the context and the content of your life."

D. A. Gregory, Sr.

In October 2006, I was a panelist for Midlevel Manager Symposium hosted by the Executive Leadership Council, where the question was asked, "Can you really or realistically have it all?" My answer to the question was, "Yes, once you define what *all* is—for you. But this act of defining *all* is difficult primarily because the definition is not static or concrete. It will change *as you change*."

As you progress along the path of this journey we call life, what was critical or crucial in your teens and in early adulthood may not be the primary drivers as you mature. Each stage of living presents unique challenges. As relationships change and levels of responsibility increase, priorities will shift.

- Question: How does one make choices in the midst of constant change?

- Answer: Focus.

A key contributor to one's success is the ability to focus. It has not always been my strong suit, but it is an acquired talent that must be cultivated in order to reap the desired benefits this life has to offer. *Webster's Dictionary* defines focus as "the center of interest or activity or an act of concentrating interest or activity on something." Other equivalent descriptions include the focal point, central point, center of attention, hub, pivot, nucleus, heart, cornerstone, linchpin, emphasis, accent, priority, concentration subject, theme, topic, issue, thesis, point, substance, the essence of the matter, the core, or one's vision. There are two key concepts I have found most helpful in understanding the benefits of focus. They are core and vision.

I like the word "core" because it is the point of convergence, the place from which the context and content of your life emanates. Whatever you determine to be the core or the focus of your life defines the context for the choices or decisions you make and, as a result, drives the things you ultimately do that become the content of your life. This fact raised some interesting and timely questions for me to answer for myself. What is core to me? What is primary to my existence? What is that which drives me? Is it my work life, my family life, my spiritual life, my social life? Is it my gender, my race, my affiliations (fraternity, sorority, political, professional)? Who am I, and how did I get this way?

Many of us know colleagues who have expressed frustration after having experienced significant emotional events, such as:

- The loss of family
- Distant or difficult relationships with family
- A blown marriage or marriages
- Tirelessly working to build a career at the expense of their most valuable relationships, only to be downsized or discarded
- An unexpected negative health diagnosis

Upon critical reflection and self-assessment, the area discovered to be their core was often the incorrect choice. They discovered they had focused on the wrong goal.

Secondly, the word "focus" also brings to mind the concept of vision. When something is in focus, it is deemed to be sharp, crisp, distinct, clear, well defined, and well focused. When something is out of focus, it is described as blurred, unfocused, fuzzy, hazy, misty, cloudy, or lacking definition. Vision is often discussed as and can be considered synonymous with the term "purpose." Many people live their entire lives without understanding their purpose. They wander through life as a sleepwalker, moving in a suppressed state of consciousness, unable to make the desired level of contribution because they are unsure or unaware of the vision or purpose intended for their lives.

What is your focus? What is core to you? What is the central point of your life? What or who is the key driver in the decisions that you make? Warning: Be careful before you answer; there may be evidence to the contrary. You may have guessed my suggestion for what *should* be the core of one's life by the title of this book. My focus is to have you arrive at that same conclusion, but lest I be guilty of trying to preach too early, keep reading.

I, like most men, buy things from time to time that require assembly. Unlike most men, however, I am mechanically challenged. So to supplement my area of weakness, I call on my neighbor Johnny, who is a man's man and knows *everything* when it comes to putting things together. One day, as opportunity would have it, I bought something—a basketball goal—and I called Johnny for his expert assistance, which he was only too willing to provide (he *did not* want to help). Upon his arrival to the house, he, of course, took over the construction process, and I was relegated to the role of apprentice. As a wise apprentice, I offered the only piece of assistance I felt would be appropriate. I offered Johnny the instructions—the manufacturer's directions for assembly. Of course, Johnny, as any self-respecting man's man would, rejected the instructions. His rationale was, "I know what I am doing here; it's just a simple basketball goal."

Many of us approach life in a similar manner. We believe we have a little inkling or insight into what we are supposed to be, just as Johnny knew what an assembled basketball goal was supposed to look like. As a result, we tend not to consult the manufacturer as to what his desired purpose is for our existence. We know what we are good at, and we tend to allow our gifts and talents, hopes or desires operate unfettered by the manufacturer's blueprint for our lives. We quickly experience the frustration that comes when somehow we don't get it quite right and have constructed a life that is different that the manufacturer intended or we encounter a malfunction that is a direct result of our headstrong, self-willed actions. It is here that most of us start to tinker frantically and make adjustments that usually serve to add insult to injury. Finally, after much wasted time and effort, the dysfunction of the situation, like a basketball goal that won't adjust to different heights, forces the humbling act of consulting the instructions to get proper direction to correct our errors.

I have found in my short forty-plus-year existence that the manufacturer intended for him and his instructions to be my focus. God's instructions serve as the context of my life. God's direction facilitates the content of my life. All he desires for me to be is directly aligned with and connected to his plan for me. How well I follow his instructions will dictate the quality of the assembly of my life. This process works best if I consult God's instructions at the beginning and throughout the development process. God has a perfect plan that, if I am willing to follow, will result in my achieving his intended plan and purpose for my life. To achieve the desired goal I must subdue my male ego (or for my female counterparts who refuse to have a man tell them what to do) or your feminist independence to believe in his vision and follow the direction he provides.

This requires *focus*, and focus requires *faith*. Good

news! That's the next chapter. By the way, we got the basketball goal up finally. Thanks, Johnny!

Faith

> "Faith is acting like a thing is so, even when it's not so, in order that it might be so."
>
> *The late Pastor Dr. E. K. Bailey*

One of the benefits of my membership at the Sharon Baptist Church of Philadelphia in the early 1990s was the opportunity to be exposed to some of the best preaching in the world. The highlight of the year for me would be when the church anniversary revival would come and the larger-than-life, Texas-sized personality of none other than Dr. Everett K. Bailey would come to town. I could gauge my growth literally year to year by where I was sitting when E. K. came.

I started out the first year in the balcony. The next year, I was in the back on the main floor. The following year, I was in the middle, near the front; the next year, I was a deacon in training, sitting on the left side of the sanctuary, right in front, at the base of the pulpit.

The following year, I was a deacon, and two years later, a minister. I was seated in the pulpit now, growing closer to God and more in awe of the gift he had given E. K. As the prominent pastor of the Concord Missionary Baptist Church, Dr. Bailey had an ego and could appear gruff or intimidating. He had a persona that was as large as Texas. He was big, brash, and bold, but once you met him and got to know him, you grew to love him, even if he was a Cowboys fan (he never let us forget).

Three things I grew to know about Dr. Bailey:

1. He loved Jesus.

2. He loved Sheila, his wife, and his children.

3. He loved preaching.

It was in the preaching moment that he shared this unforgettable quote regarding faith. He said, "Faith is acting like a thing is so, even when it's not so, in order that it might be so."

I am sure it was not the first time it was said. It is possible that he is not the originator of the quote, but for me, it has remained the most practical contemporary definition or illustration of faith I have come upon. After all, for many of us faith can be a difficult attribute to exhibit. In fact, it is my unfortunate conclusion that "we talk by faith and walk by sight." We settle to believe only what we see and reduce God to a Sunday-morning feel-good created by an inspirational song or sermon, prayer or proclamation. True faith is so much more, but it requires some things from you.

Now, if you are not willing to participate in this transformational process, go hit the DVR and catch up on whatever it is you watch. But if you desire to grow your faith, there are at least three things I need to share with you: Faith is optional, faith is operational, and faith is opportunistic.

Faith Is Optional

Faith is unique. It is a noun, a thing, but you can't see it. It is something that you cannot be double minded about; either you have it or you don't. But it is optional because it is *your choice*. *What do you mean?* I'm glad you asked!

Faith is a byproduct of a trust relationship. Whatever or whoever you have established a relationship of trust with is where you will place your faith. Faith is optional because only you can choose with whom or what you will have a trust relationship. This is particularly true with God. He desires to have a relationship with us based on trust, and from Genesis to Revelation, God reiterates this point. He does not, however, force us to have a relationship. Jesus is the perfect gentleman, standing at the door, gently knocking, and then he stands patiently waiting, hoping for us to invite him in. It is our choice whether we even believe in God, and many of us claim to believe, but our actions don't back up our words.

In fact, in life, many of us stand paralyzed like a nervous golfer over a short three-foot putt. You see the ball, the line, and know all you need to do is take it straight back and follow through. But there you stand—palms sweating, eyes squinting, and *you miss!* Why? Is it because you don't trust your putter? No. Is it because you have not spent the time practicing your short putts? No. You missed before you ever struck the ball because you didn't believe you would make it! You have to visualize the putt going in and strike it confidently, trusting the read and the stroke. That is why I (and everyone else who loves golf) love to watch Tiger Woods putt. The way he studies, stands over, and strokes a putt makes you feel like he is going to make it every time. Whether he ultimately makes it or misses the putt is not as important as the fact that he actually believes he can make it, and more often than not, when it counts, he does because he chose to believe.

Faith Is Operational

The Bible is so clear on this point: Faith without works is dead. The evidence that your faith is living or operational is the actions that are birthed of it. The very validation that you have faith is the fact that you move beyond lip service to tangible effort. It is the actual effort that transforms vision into reality. You might ask, *Why is this important?* The ability to activate or make your faith operational will often, if not always, be the differentiating factor that allows you to achieve your dreams. While "faith without works is dead" is a very familiar verse, it is often most difficult to live. So many dreams are buried with the dreamer because he or she never woke up and put forth the effort to achieve the goal.

One of my favorite movies is *The Untouchables* with a star-studded cast including Kevin Costner as Elliot Ness, Andy Garcia as a young detective, and the incomparable Sean Connery as the old Irish beat cop who shows young Elliot how to dismantle Al Capone's (played by Robert

DeNiro) illegal liquor operations. I grew up watching the old television series reruns, so I was excited when I heard it was being made into a movie.

The most riveting scene was when was when Frank Nitty gunned down the old beat cop (Connery) in his home. As he lay on the floor riddled with bullets, blood gushing from his mortal wounds, he starts to crawl across the floor to get to the key he needs to give to Elliot Ness. But when Elliot gets there and finds his friend near death, the old cop sees the fear registered in the young man's eyes and senses the possibility that he may pull back and even quit thinking the price too high to fight Capone. But with his last raspy, blood-filled gasps, he reaches up and grabs Elliot and asks him a simple but profound question, which would determine whether the old cop's life had been sacrificed in vain: "What are you prepared to do?"

The old cop knew that faith is not the talk of the converted but the actions of the committed.

Faith Is Opportunistic

Once you move in faith, you will discover a unique phenomenon: God will position resources and opportunities along the journey that will serve in bringing your dream to reality. He uses both good and bad to work together to facilitate his plan for your life.

- I was downsized once, and I started my own company, Genesis Consulting, a small business-consulting firm, and guess what! I got clients!

- I developed a business plan for a restaurant concept and, with no prior experience, almost landed a restaurant.

- I got fired from a job because I refused to compromise my integrity, and the door was opened for me to become the first-ever deputy auditor general for the Commonwealth of Pennsylvania.

- On the recommendation of a faithful friend, I answered the call of a headhunter and became the youngest vice president for a multibillion-dollar health insurer.

I could go on and on, but if you are flipping the pages of this book, you are directly participating in the latest God-inspired success in my life; you bought my book! Whether you deem it foolish or faith filled, if you are willing to act on the promptings of God, you can do anything! The reason I say that faith is opportunistic is that opportunity only presents itself to those who are willing to do something.

A song in the gospel world made popular by the Miami Mass Choir declares, "What God has for me, it is for me." But what the songwriter fails to say is, if you do nothing, what God has for you he will keep or give to someone else, someone who is willing to exhibit enough faith to move!

The story is told of the young woman who saw and answered the advertisement for a job in a new company that had moved to her town. She was invited in for an interview, and the interview went so well that the company indicated they would be in touch shortly. The young woman, filled with excitement, rushed home to tell her mother the anticipated good news, believing she had gotten the job. Her mother was overjoyed for her daughter's good news, also believing that she had gotten the job she had been praying for. Each day the young lady would get dressed and wait for the mail to arrive, hurriedly running down to the mailbox to see if the letter announcing the job had come. Days passed but no letter. Days became weeks, weeks became months, but no letter. The young lady kept up the faith dutifully, expectantly waiting for the letter. But after two months of no contact, the mother, thinking her daughter's ritual of going to the mailbox day after day to be futile, could no longer hold her peace. "Why do you continue to look for this letter? Isn't it obvious to you that the company chose someone else? Face the facts. The job's not coming."

Just as Mama finished her sentence, the delivery truck pulled up in the front of the house. "Special delivery!" yelled the postman. The daughter went to door and signed for the letter-sized package. All of a sudden, euphoric sounds erupted from porch. "Mama! Mama!" Her mother came running, unsure of what had just happened. The daughter, full of joy, announced, "I got the job! I got the job!"

She handed her mother the letter from the senior vice president of human resources that indicated she had indeed gotten the job and should call his office immediately upon receipt.

When she called, the good news got better!

The SVP informed her that there had been an oversight. The offer letter was supposed to have gone out two months earlier. So in light of their error, she would receive back pay for the two months. In addition, the position had been reevaluated, and the salary she would be receiving would be 20 percent higher! Now this is where E. K. would have celebrated in the cultural tradition of the African-American Baptist preacher and hollered, "Faith is acting like a thing is so, even when it's not so, in order that it might be so!"

    To *trust* God requires faith.
    Problem: You cannot trust in a God you *do not* know.
    To *know* God requires fellowship.
    Problem Solved: Next chapter–"Fellowship"

Fellowship

> Question: What is the one thing you spend without knowing how much was put in your account or how much you have left?
> Answer: Time!

A key economic concept that has universal application is return on investment (ROI). The concept of ROI addresses the fact that any investor who makes an investment of value has the expectation of a return. In fact, the greater the investment, the greater the expectation of a return. God is no different. In us he has made an investment. He has given us life, he has entrusted us with talents, he has given us resources, and all he asks in return is a simple commodity—time.

Time with God

Now, on the surface it seems easy, but finding time for God seems to be a struggle for many. *Why do we struggle* (yes, I said *we*)? I'm glad you asked. We struggle because we do not value the relationship appropriately. We do not value the relationship appropriately because we do not understand with whom we are in relationship. As a result, we do not prioritize him in our lives. If we understood who it is that desires to spend time with us, and the benefits to be derived from spending time with him, we would rearrange our priorities.

When I was pursuing my spouse, I made it a point to prioritize her in tangible ways. I made time for her in my schedule and put spending time with her above the time I had been spending in other more trivial pursuits. Why? It was because I was getting a return on my investment. The reason our relationship is as successful as it is because I have continued to make investments of time (and treasure) to convey her importance to me, and she has continued to let me know my attention is valued.

Importance can also be expressed as intimacy. Now, I like to play with words, so I break down the word "intimacy" as *in-to-me-see*. I make my investment in my wife not because of what I am going to get out of our relationship but because of who she is in my life. Because I communicate through my spending time with her that I am into her, I get the desired response that says she is *in-to-me-see*, and I am motivated to make greater investments.

Another companion benefit is that because I have made deposits, or investments, I can make withdrawals. In times of trouble, I can make withdrawals of support and reassurance. In times of discouragement, I can make withdrawals of compassion and strength and she likewise. But in those seasons when we take each other for granted and allow life to push us into a routine where we neglect or ignore each other, the intimacy is interrupted because the absence of fellowship has impaired our connection. What does this have to do with me and my relationship with God? Everything.

Oftentimes our relationship with God can be flawed in its motivation. If the relationship is not valued on the basis of who he is as opposed to what we want or need, the relationship becomes warped, and we struggle because our communication with God breaks down. We are good at talking like we have an intimate relationship with God, especially when our money's right, our relationships are tight, your bankroll is fat, and the talk amongst friends is that you're all that! But when you are busted and disgusted, "tore up from the floor up," and our fair-weather friends have deserted us, our testimony often drowns in the sea of complaining. I am learning that the value of my verbal testimony about who God is to me is not found in the comfort of the calm periods in my life but in the midst of the storm. My belief in God is most evident in how I respond when things are not going well and my victorious living gives way to the valley experience. Said another way, the value of our verbal testimony is validated by our response during the times we are tested.

To take a page out of my own experience, I was lying in bed one morning, depressed and discouraged about a recent job transition. It seemed like my professional networks had all shut down and nobody was calling. My feelings ranged from anger to disappointment, and I felt forgotten. All my plans seemed to be on hold or on life support. We were experiencing personal tests and family challenges, and I felt there was no one I could or wanted to talk to. To top it off, I was struggling to write this book, this particular chapter. So, as I sat groggily one morning in my bedroom in the midst of my personal pity party, I noticed there sat a book with a missing cover. I picked up the book but did not open it and laid it on the side of the tub. Out of my sleep-filled eyes I happened to see, lying there in the magazine basket, the tattered cover sitting inside out. I bent over and picked up the cover, flipped it over quickly, and wrapped it around the book. It was then that I recognized the title.

- It was a devotional Bible.

- It was a devotional Bible entitled *Time with God*.

- It was a devotional Bible entitled *Time with God* that was available to me every morning.

- It was a devotional Bible entitled *Time with God* that was available to me every evening.

- The book represented a message from our God, who is available to you and me every morning, every evening, even in the midnight hour.

- The book represented a message from a loving God who is waiting to be invited to share in our ups and downs, high and lows, our disappointments and grief.

Then it hit me! The book was an illustration of what I was missing in my own life. I was missing our fellowship.

I was missing my time with God. What about you? He is not just a good God in good times but at all times. He really is "good all the time and all the time, God is good!" However, to have that as your testimony, it requires that you cultivate a relationship with God. That requires the investment of time.

Your Testimony about God

My wife and children run into problems from time to time. Now, despite their complaints that I occasionally fuss when they have these problems (I don't know what they are talking about), they still come to me when they inevitably have them. Why is that? Could it be my track record? Even though I may fuss, they know three things:

- I care (more than I let on sometimes)
- I can relate (been there, done that)
- I come through with the help they require (usually)

This knowledge about their past issues and the history of how I tried to help them provides the basis for their testimony in regards to dealing with Dad. It works the same way with God.

If you are going to be successful in dealing with the issues, problems, and challenges of life, you need to know you can call on a God who will answer and is able to do something about your situation. Many of us experience a higher degree of anxiety than necessary because our memory is flawed when it comes to God's track record. In fact, we should take a closer look at the word "memory." Memory is defined in *Webster's Dictionary* as the power or process of reproducing or recalling what has been learned or retained, especially through associative mechanisms. What's that mean, and how does it relate to me? Good question.

It means that through your association with God and spending time with God, you should be able to remember situations where you called on God and how he moved to facilitate your success. But our memory is flawed; therefore, in times of trouble, we default to our fears. We rehearse in our minds everything that could go wrong, which only serves to magnify our fears. When you live *life in the key of G*, you will experience fear, but your association with God should pull up the plasma screen of your mind and allow you to remember your past and see the victories that God has won on your behalf.

Instead of complaining or rehearsing your concession speech to the problems in your life, you can say as King David said, "I have been young and now I am old; yet I have never seen the righteous forsaken, nor his descendents begging bread" (Psalm 37:25, NKJV). David leverages the positive memories of his tenure with God, understanding it will produce positive results in his inner thinking, which will positively affect his outward communication. Take note of Psalms 34:1–2 (NKJV): "I will bless the LORD at all times, His praise shall continually be in my mouth. My soul shall make its boast in the LORD, the humble shall hear of it and be glad" (NKJV). His communication not only serves to encourage him, but the others who are watching and hearing his response, even while he is dealing with his situation, are encouraged by his perspective. David doesn't stop there; he invites us all to participate in the life-altering power of praise and worship in Psalm 34:3: "O magnify the LORD with me and let us exalt His name together" (NKJV). David's perspective is not contingent on his condition but a reflection of his communion with God.

TALKING (DIALOGUE) WITH GOD

A key benefit that fellowship with God brings in a successful life is the anticipation of the intervention of an almighty, all-powerful God in the midst of my circumstances. When the old Baptist preacher exclaims, "When I think of the goodness of Jesus and all he's done for me," he is trying to get the congregation to remember how God has provided in the past and encourage them with the fact that he is still just a prayer away!

When you spend time with God, you build a history with God that you can access anytime, anywhere. A divine benefit of being in fellowship with God is the ability to talk with God and have him talk back to you. One of the key foundations to any relationship is communication. It is paramount that if there is to be evidence of fellowship, there must be contact, not just a cursory exchange, but intimate contact. The most successful individuals I know are not the ones who have the largest offices, the deepest pockets, or most impressive titles, but, in fact, are the ones who enjoy an intimate, consistent, abiding relationship with God. How is your prayer life? What is on the mind of God for your life? Have you asked him? I am sure you have told him what is on your mind for your life, but is the relationship a two-way street or a congested one-way highway? The reason I ask these questions is because I am coming to better understand the component of prayer called *listening*.

I am known for being talkative, and at times I am out of balance when it comes to listening versus talking. It was a communication blind spot that hindered my being more effective in communications with others. This imbalance between my listening and my talking caused others to tune out because it did not seem that I valued their contribution to the dialogue. Now, if this can happen in a human context, imagine God, who already knows what you need, having to sit and listen as you bombard the throne of grace with your laundry list of requests, waiting patiently for you to let him speak. Then, when it is his turn, you don't even return the courtesy and listen to him. Wow!

Fellowship facilitates communion. Communion describes a mutual relationship where interests, activities, feelings, and experiences are shared for the good of both parties. God wants to hear from you but also wants you to hear from him. Part of talking to God involves reading and meditating on God's Word. The psalmist David underscored the benefit of listening to the right influences and its direct correlation to your success. Listen to these words:

> Blessed is the man that walks not in the counsel of the ungodly, nor stands in the ways of sinners nor sits in the seat of the scornful; But his delight is in the law of the Lord and in His Word does he meditate day and night. And he

> shall be like a tree; planted by the rivers of water that brings forth its fruit in its season. Its leaf also shall not wither and whatsoever he does shall prosper.
>
> Psalm 1:1–3 (NKJV)

Learning this lesson is key to your success. It's not spooky; in fact, it's simple. Literally, when you open your Bible, God opens his mouth to make his thoughts and his desires for your life known to you. The spirit of God through meditation on his Word makes clear the direction, actions, and purpose for your life. When it comes to fellowship and talking with God, the successful man or woman recognizes whose words hold the most value. My former pastor, Bishop Keith W. Reed, Sr., said it this way, "I would rather hear God's Word without your comments than your comments without God's Word."

No relationship will ever compare to the one we cultivate with God. Recent best-selling books like *Your Best Life Now* by Joel Osteen, *A Purpose Driven Life* by Rick Warren, and *Developing the Leader Within* by John Maxwell all leverage biblical principles to express and validate the life-changing concepts they present. They each acknowledge the critical need for a closer relationship with God. No new age philosophy or self-help tutorial that makes you the central focus will ever bring the satisfaction that a life surrendered to God will bring. Until we improve our relationship with God, all other relationships have little chance of being successful. After all, our true purpose, the reason we were created, the reason we exist, is for fellowship with God.

Horizontal Orientation

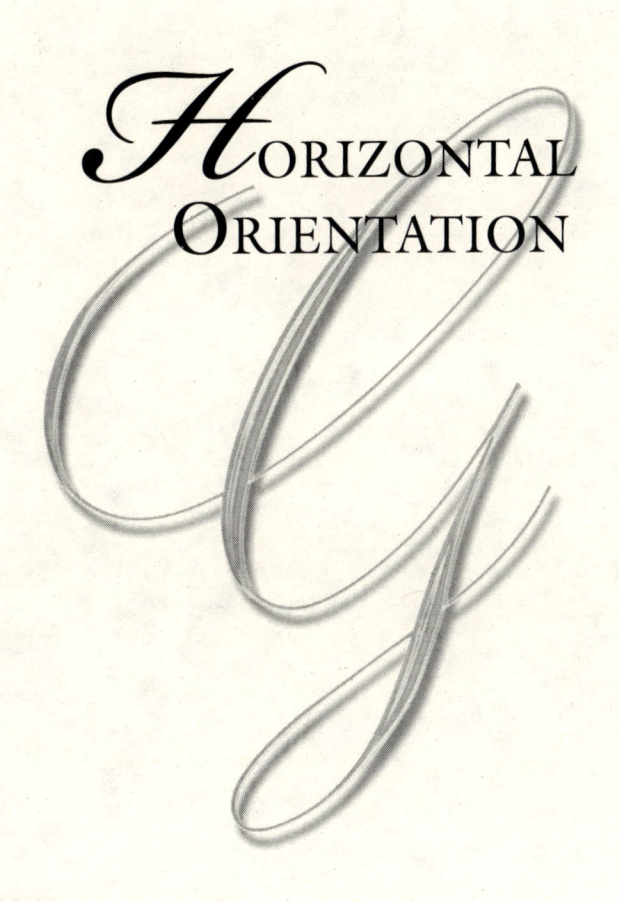

Family

> "A truth, that of which I am sure, is after God, nothing matters more than family."
>
> *D. A. Gregory, Sr.*

I have a number of things I am known for; the one thing, however, that seems to have the greatest impact on those I meet is my personal statistics. Let me share some and you see what jumps out at you.

- I have one house.
- I have three cars.
- I have seven credit cards (six too many).
- Okay, I have about fifteen suits (my one vice).
- I have one wife.
- We have been married twenty-three years.

- We have been blessed with six wonderful children and a handsome grandson.

Six children! Yeah, I hear you as your mind comes to a screeching halt. Six! Then come the questions about my religious affiliation. Are you Catholic? (This question really warms the heart of this Baptist preacher.) The more comical acquaintance usually asks if we know how "this" (reproduction) happens. But for the most part, the "six children" part tends to leave the hearer awestruck. They usually pause mentally to momentarily project themselves into my situation and contemplate what it would feel like to have six children and promptly proceed to run like heck back to serenity of their 2.4-kid comfort zone.

Most women quickly elevate my wife to sainthood and relegate me to sinner status. Many comment about how they struggle with their particular allotment of children and could not see the way to have that many kids. The questions range from how can we afford to have that many kids to how do my wife and I find time for each other? Others make certain comments that I am sure sound cute in their mind but leave my wife and me wondering how someone managed to get God to put their backside where their mouth belongs.

The real deal is that no matter if you have ten children, one, or none, family matters. Family matters to God.

First Things First: Marriage

Let's start where God started. In the beginning, the first relationship God instituted was marriage. He made

Adam and Eve and commanded that they would be the prototype relationship model. They were ocular demonstrations of God's perfect plan as they met each other's needs by enjoying the key aspects of the marital relationship—companionship, communication, recreation, and procreation. How do these work? I am glad you asked. Let's take a deeper dive and see.

COMPANIONSHIP: FALLING IN "LIKE" WITH EACH OTHER.

"It was not good for man to be alone" was God's observation, so God created someone suitable as a helpmate. He created woman to fill the void. God was so clear in his intentions that it should eliminate any other alternative relationship possibility. And since God never makes mistakes, his original intent is the only orientation worthy of consideration.

If you are going to fill that void, you need to find someone suitable for you. Eve was tailor made by God for Adam. Someone is being tailor-made for you too, but your mate is not necessarily going to be *like* you. In fact, he or she that God has ordained is not supposed to be like you. He or she is meant to be *complementary* to you. That is why dating is so dangerous. During the dating process or courtship, we attempt to drown our individuality to become this pretend person someone else can fall in love with, only to pull a bait and switch once married. This is called making a permanent decision based on temporary conditions.

Many couples have relationships that are failing because they fell in love (last time I checked, falling is normally painful) and failed to like each other. Many of our relationships are dominated by a focus from the waist down and never do a "checkup from the neck up." If you had, you could have discerned that your current mate was crazy prior to saying "I do." Now, the foggy delusion of sexual bliss has worn off, and you clearly do not know the person with whom you have pledged to spend the rest of your life. Hopefully, you are single while reading this and can avoid the mistakes of some our parents, siblings, and peers. The foundation of a successful family is built on the bond of marital friendship.

Communication: Before You Get Married

If your goal is to navigate your way to the marriage altar with the person of your dreams, I have some rules, recommendations, or, perhaps, requirements that I believe God will back me up on through his Word.

For the men:

1. *Environmental security*: A woman needs to know that you can provide a safe place for her. This is not necessarily limited to an economic assessment because the woman in your life or of your dreams may have the economic resources to provide comfortably for herself or you both, but she can't be *her own man*. A man provides an atmosphere of safety and stability when he is around. Does she feel better, safer, more secure when you are around? Does her burden get lighter

when she can see you in the room or hold your hand and hear your voice?

2. *Learn to lead biblically*: If she is considering submitting to your leadership, she needs to know exactly whom it is that you are following. The quickest way to *live life off-key* is to follow a man who does not know who "G" (God) is.

3. *Prioritize friendship—spend time having fun*: Friendship between couples is such an underrated component of today's relationships. Doing fun things like bowling, dancing, watch the game, movies, group dates, or shows; even shopping at the mall create opportunities to get to know her better. Instead of investing time to become friends, relationships often start with lust, which is mistaken for love. Unfortunately, in many relationships, friendship is the caboose on the train when, in fact, it is the engine of most successful relationships. You want a woman who you like as a friend because when I like you, it is easy to love you.

4. *Develop listening skills*: Master the ability to listen and hear what she is saying. Part of growing the relationship is the ability to read between the lines. A woman will try and communicate things subtly to try and protect your fragile male ego. Do not miss the message! Invest time together to facilitate an atmosphere where open and honest

dialogue is welcomed and embraced. Your ego may suffer a bruise or two, but your friendship and relationship will flourish.

5. *Treat her like a diamond*: I have had the pleasure of purchasing a few diamonds for my wife of twenty-plus years (she lost the first one and cried for days). I've noticed on my shopping trips that jewelers never attempt to sell me on a diamond by focusing my attention on the flaws; they always draw my attention to the diamond's facets. The jeweler shines the diamond so that it can be seen in its best light. So it should be with the person you desire to spend the rest of your life with. I know she has flaws; so do you! If you fix some of yours, it may reduce or eliminate hers.

For the Women:

1. *Take your time and let him find you*: The Bible says in Proverbs 18:22 (NKJV), "He who finds a wife finds a good thing." When a man expresses an interest in a woman and her feeling is mutual, she should try to resist the urge to go window-shopping at the bridal store on the first date. That may be perceived as scary and just a bit premature. The microwave works well for late-night popcorn, not for long-term relationships.

2. *Be everything you want*: So many times the expectations that women put on Mr. Right

are so high that few men, if any, can truly be all that. But on the outside chance that he does exist, I have a question: Would he want you? Are you able to live up to the criteria that you have established for him? Can you meet your own standard? Can you meet God's standard for what a woman should be? *Shh!* Don't answer.

3. *Do not excuse bad behavior*: So many battered women's shelters, hospitals, and graveyards are full of women who allowed, tolerated, or excused abuse. I don't care what the socio-economic, political benefits are or what the outer package looks like. I know too many stories of abused women who saw it coming or failed to expose the abuse in its infancy, accepting some flimsy apology that wore off as soon as he got mad about something else. Abuse in a dating relationship is an immediate and absolute deal breaker. Don't cover it up, don't excuse it, and please do not ignore it.

4. *Don't settle*: As Christians, you and your faith should be inseparable! You require a companion who shares your beliefs. I have often asked the question of Christian ladies as to whether their prospective mate is saved. The response I get back is, "Well, he goes to church with me sometimes." That answer is usually an indicator that she has decided to settle and become "unevenly

yoked," which will have negative consequences downstream in the relationship.

5. *Adopt a Ruth Chris versus a Sam's Club mentality regarding pre-marital intimacy*: If someone asked you for a chance to "sample" you sexually, you would, at minimum, probably be offended; however, some of today's dating and relationship standards suggest a "Sam's Club" mentality. Let me explain. At Sam's Club, in order to entice you to buy a particular product, they give away free samples. This is not the best protocol for dating. I suggest one employ a Ruth Chris standard: I have had the rare occasion to dine at Ruth Chris, and I noticed it had an air of exclusivity. One thing I did not observe, however, was a steak-sampling station in the lobby. In order to dine there, one must be able to pay full price for the experience. If there is a man who desires to know you in an intimate way, do not allow yourself to "sampled," but rather answer him in the words of Sasha Fierce (aka Beyonce), "If you like it than you ought to put a ring on it... uh, uh, oh."

COMMUNICATION: NOW THAT YOU'RE MARRIED

From time to time, my wife and I will do perform marital counseling or facilitate marital retreats, and as part of breaking the ice, we will have couples take part in a sensitivity exercise. We ask them to remember how they met. This is a fun exercise that often causes the room to fill with laughter, *oohs* and *aahs* as couples share their stories. I ask things like: "Who made the first move?" and, "What did he or she do that closed the deal to make you know that this person would be the one?"

These questions take couples back to a happy time, a time when they were both trying really hard to put their best foot forward, to be sensitive to their potential life partner's needs. Having each couple remember and retell the selfless, romantic, seemingly corny, or even silly actions that were performed to get their spouse's attention to the other couples in attendance is so powerful because it helps all the couples remember why they fell in love in the first place. Do you remember how you felt when you fell in love?

See, now that you're married, those feelings can get smothered by the daily grind. Our marriages often take on the beautiful color of battleship gray and contain all the excitement of a cold bowl of half-eaten oatmeal left on a kitchen counter. Or could it be, now that you are married, the real you has shown up and your relationship is facing challenges. Don't deny it! Whether married for minutes, months, or millenniums, we all face marital challenges.

Challenges Create Irritation—Irritation results from the friction caused oftentimes because we address issues in our relationship without God's Word. This leaves us to respond through our carnal mind rather than the spirit-filled wisdom that God provides through his Holy Spirit. As a result, we cause significant, often irreparable, damage to our mates because of ill-spoken words and malicious actions that stem from poor judgment and anger.

Pencils come with erasers; tongues do not! Successful relationships employ the wisdom that says, "Be quick to hear, slow to speak, slow to anger" (James 1:21, NKJV).

Challenges Can Cause Insensitivity–Men can be particularly given to this trait. Your wife has a profound need for attention. This need is often manifested in her desire to talk, to be reaffirmed, to be acknowledged, and to be pampered. At times, we men can be very rude because we tend not to be as needy in this area, and so we consider it to be nagging. But you set her up!

You were the same guy who would talk for hours about nothing just to let her know that you cared. Yeah, you did! Now you expect her to fit her concerns in between halftime or commercials. You take her out, and you don't open doors, don't compliment her, and don't pay, and then come home and have the audacity to want some! Your game is raggedy, playa! Marriage has the same motto as the ATM machine: "No deposit, no return!"

Challenges Erode Intimacy–The intimacy that you experienced during the courtship has given way to the arctic breeze of indifference. In fact, men have increasingly confided that wives have relegated the sexual experience to Father's Day, Christmas, birthdays, and anniversaries. That is crazy! The Bible states, with the exception of a mutually agreed-upon time for prayer and fasting, that you and your spouse ought to be rendering due benevolence to each other all the time. When you weren't married, some of you were fornicating all the time, and now that you have a legitimate relationship, you play games and sex is a bartering chip in many relationships, used primarily for manipulation. If you do not want your man getting drunk on the bootleg wine of extramarital affairs available in the street, you would be wise to let him get drunk on the wine of your love at home! And brother, if you're too busy working or have your attention where it does not belong, you may find that the wife you ignore is the woman of someone else's dreams. It's tight, but it's right!

Most marital and relationship challenges stem from poor communication. Poor communication erodes commitment. When you defraud each other sexually, you open the door for temptation to draw either you or both of you into illicit relationships, both mental and physical, that can poison your relationship. A successful marriage in the *key of G* requires intimacy.

COMMITMENT: 'TIL DEATH DO YOU PART

To be successful in the secular pursuits of this world and fail at family is a tragedy, yet in our scandal-ridden society many are guilty of this failure. I, too, would be counted among life's casualties if I had not had the benefits of role models and mentors who pulled me back from following the foolishness of momentary pleasure. I learned that in the world of the sacred, the ability to successfully manage family was a prerequisite for consideration for any office of significance. A man who desired to serve in the house of God must rule his own house and rule it well.

Now, it is amazing how we in the church have disdain for the antics of the world, but, unfortunately, we in the church, like the men who were ready to stone the woman caught in adultery, are equally as guilty. From the parking lot to the pulpit and from the pulpit to the pews, we in the church have fallen short of God's intended representation of marriage. Our willingness to exemplify commitment is at an all-time low. The divorce rate among Christians is staggering, and many couples that remain together struggle to stay the course. The marriage commitment between a man and a woman is supposed to be a reflection of the sacrificial love that Christ displays to his church. Commitment in marriage today is anything but.

One major contributing factor to the failures is the self-centered, commercially oriented mind-set we bring to the marital relationship. Whether it is the celebrity-studded weddings of Star Jones or Juanita Bynum or the latest reality wedding show that gets behind the scenes to show all the drama and nonsense that goes into making the bride's day perfect, marriage has been getting a bad rap, and it's getting worse. All the focus is on the size of the bling, carats in the ring, and the hype that, at the end of the day, is much ado about nothing. Why? Because the planning lasted longer than the marriage! That's why! The external energy and expense wasted on impressing others would have been better spent on a gift for the pastor after attending some premarital counseling and spending time developing their relationship. It would have allowed them to become lovers and stay friends. Marriage is not about having your day; it's about sharing your lives as two become one.

Climate Control: Creating the Atmosphere for Growth– As a husband and a father, I can testify that my greatest achievements and greatest joys come from seeing my wife and my children happy. I learned through a unique illustration in a sermon by my former pastor, Bishop Keith

Reed, about creating the proper atmosphere for growth. In Psalm 128, David describes some characteristics of the blessed man by metaphorically describing his wife as a fruitful vine and his children as olive plants. Let me unpack this for you.

Both olive plants and vines, normally associated with growing grapes, were used to produce olive oil and wine. Both grapes and olives grow best in stable climates. Places like northern California, France, and Italy are known for being regions that have moderate climates and are among the largest producers of olive oil and wine in the world. The home is another place that needs to have a moderate climate to promote growth. What do I mean by that?

Many of our homes suffer from climates that are too volatile. Some of your houses run much too cold, and some run much too hot. And the temperature is volatile, changing, literally, at the drop of a hat! The heat comes from anger and harshness, and the cold comes from lack of affection and attention. I have been guilty of both, so if you can't admit your failings in this area, at least learn from mine.

The Fireplace:—I am uniquely configured. I have my mother's temperament and my father's temper. Early in my marriage, I would often overreact to what I know now to be trivial issues and let my fiery temper get the best of me. I confided this dysfunction to an older gentleman who shared an illustration with me that I never forgot. He asked me, "Do you know what a fireplace is?"

"Yes," I answered.

"Did you know the purpose of fire in the fireplace?" he asked.

"To keep the house warm," I responded.

He asked yet another question: "What happens if the fire gets outside the fireplace?"

"The house would catch on fire and burn down."

"Thus endeth the lesson, grasshopper," he said.

He was letting me know that it is my responsibility to manage my passions. Getting passionate, even angry, at times, is a reality of relationship. It is important, however, to set boundaries for those passions to ensure they don't damage the relationship in an unintended, unnecessary, or even abusive manner.

Ignoring or blowing by those boundaries is the cause for significant damage in marital and parent-child relationships. Even sibling relationships are tarnished as they heap on each other the angry dysfunction they observe at home and then carry into their own marital and parenting relationships. Break the cycle!

When we exercise the appropriate restraint or table a matter until cooler heads prevail, it will allow for focus on the issues centric to the moment. It will also teach our children the emotion management skills they need to be successful in their lives.

The Icebox—Another byproduct of mismanaging the climate of the home comes in the form of keeping the environment too cool. This can happen for a variety of reasons.

- It can be the erosion of affection resulting from a pattern of neglect that has eroded the goodwill of the mate to the point of indifference. For example, this often happens with a spouse who, after years of worrying if an unfaithful husband would come home and whom he was with, no longer cares.

- It also happens with husbands who have wives who schedule sex like a quarterly conference call or believe that headscarves, facial creams, and flannel pajamas every night are the equivalent of Viagra. It is not!

- Or maybe you are the verbally abusive or complaining spouse or parent who now is just tuned out and ignored by a mate or tuned out by children who have resigned themselves to never being able to please you and no longer care to make the effort. They are happiest when you pull out of the driveway to leave the house and saddest when you return, oftentimes pensive, not sure if Dr. Jekyll or Mr. (or Mrs.) Hyde is returning.

- Or could you be the preoccupied spouse who is externally focused on your career and have prioritized other things while you miss the important moments in your children's life, deluding yourself into believing you are sacrificing so they can have a better life?

Newsflash: They don't want a better life; they want a life with you! But if you wait too long or make too many excuses, they will be disappointed, dismayed, disinterested, and probably feel just plain dissed by the time you pencil them into your world.

Your wife or husband is not some trophy to be dusted off from time to time or a ball and chain of obligation with whom you go through the perfunctory motions to have an occasional conversationless, boring dinner. You've seen those couples (you may be those couples) who sit with long stretches of silence as they try to remember how they got to this arctic moment in their relationship. No! Don't be them! Be better than that! You can do it!

As I said at the beginning, family matters! Husband and wives need to make each other the priority of their lives. Children need to see you laughing, kissing, caressing (PG, of course), dating, and liking each other. The children need you both involved in the scholastic, social, recreational, and, most importantly, spiritual aspects of their lives—not just telling them how to be family but also showing them that family matters *every day!*

The unfortunate reality is that if you are a poor father, your son will likely be just like you. If you are a poor husband, it is likely, despite her desire not to, that she will pick a man just like her daddy. If you are a poor mother, your children will know it, and your husband will show it. Stop the cycle! Remember why you got married, why you had children, the type of parents you wanted to be, and give your children *your best you*. It will make a profound difference in their lives.

Of this I am sure, because family matters.

Friends

> "Friends; how many of us have them?
> Friends; the kind we can depend on."
>
> *Whodini*

Friendship is a term that I do not take lightly. The unfortunate fact is that the longer I live, the more I find that the circle of friends I once cast so broad has proven to be so much smaller. That's because real friendship requires a level of character, commitment, and courage that is uncommon yet unmistakable.

I am a member of an organization whose motto is "Friendship is essential to the soul." This motto of the Omega Psi Phi fraternity is near and dear to my heart. In fraternal and ministerial circles, the biblical account of the friendship of David and Jonathan in 1 Samuel 18 is often referenced as the supreme model of friendship. But the Bible story in the Gospel of Mark 2:1–5 of four men who took a paralytic man to see Jesus is an illustration so exemplary of what successful friendship looks like, I want us to take a closer look.

I would like to highlight three unique traits that I believe to be key elements of successful or real friendships. Sisters, many of the illustrations I use in this chapter will be birthed primarily out of the relationships I have had with men; however, the traits and truths highlighted will be universal in their relevance and their application.

1. A Real Friend Is Moved by Compassion for You

My renaissance in Christ has been fueled by my involvement in men's ministry. I love being around the brothers—real men who are seeking God and desire to be more effective in their service. One of the phenomenal observations over my past twenty years of participation in men's ministry is to watch the development of trust. When men first come, they are closed. They do not just come in and start sharing their most intimate problems or secrets. That phenomenon does not occur until trust is established. The primary way to establish this trust is through demonstrating compassion.

Compassion is a trait that simply indicates that once I am aware of your situation, I don't judge you and reject you or mark you and then out you, telling your business as the latest juicy piece of gossip. No, in this setting of men, a man will find other men who, without hesitation, will move to express to this man that they've been there and they care.

See, many of us have been damaged and at some point needed some help. Oftentimes, a man may have let his guard down to express his vulnerability, and his trust was betrayed, so he locks away his trust in a place few can find (this is similar for women). Often the place where this trust can be reestablished is in the unique setting of the men's ministry. Most of my closest relationships came from the men in the ministry circles I have been privileged to participate.

In the story of the paralytic man, we find one who is broken. His physical dysfunction and disability provide the provocation necessary to motivate four of his friends to show extraordinary compassion. There is no record of a discussion between the four friends as to why or how the man became paralyzed, only actions directed at solving his situation. Each man gets personally involved in assuming responsibility for shouldering the burden of this broken brother. I believe that a true friend does not see his or her broken brother or sister in need and sit on the sidelines of life hoping someone else shows up to provide the needed assistance. No! The first thing a real friend does is show that he or she cares by doing that something to help meet that need! The saying goes that people don't care how much you know until they know how much you care. Actions speak louder than words!

2. A Real Friend Is Moved Beyond Convenience for You

Often in the process of trying to do a good deed for someone else, obstacles come our way. These impediments often come at the most inconvenient of times. Just as you see the goal or the possibility of achieving the objective that you set out for, *blam*! Something comes up to try and set you back. In our chosen illustration, as these men carry their friend to Peter's house, the place where Jesus was, it was noted that the word had already leaked out that Jesus was in town. This caused the outbreak of an impromptu citywide revival. All roads led to Peter's house; everyone tried to get to see or hear Jesus. So as the men rounded the corner to Peter's house, their destination in sight, they ran smack into the burgeoning, standing-room-only crowd surrounding the place where Jesus was preaching.

This obstacle could have been the catalyst for aborting the mission. After all, how many of us, after carrying a man across town only to find that the crowd blocked the door, would have packed it in? We would have expressed our regret to the crippled man, acknowledging that we did our best, but we couldn't get him to the desired destination because it is inconvenient. After all, they did their best; certainly, they did more than most. They did make a sacrifice to carry him a long way. No one could fault them because they at least tried to help. Sound familiar? I mean, hey, if you put your leftover change in the counter receptacle left by whichever charity is collecting that month or drop some change to the street person who is down on his luck, who can complain? If you give to the United Way, March of Dimes, the American Red Cross, or charity of your choosing, should not that be enough? I am not saying not to do these things, but I do suggest that they represent the way of convenience. When you get involved in the life of your friends, especially when they are going through the storms of life, you may find yourself getting wet, because storms seem to break out when they don't have an umbrella around. This is when God will use you or me to be that umbrella to provide the necessary support or shelter for a friend. These four men did not turn around and take their broken friend back home in the same impotent condition, but instead they moved beyond convenience to model another facet of successful friendship.

3. A Real Friend Is Moved with Conviction for You

The story continues in the most unlikely manner, because our next scene finds the four men and the paralytic man up on the roof. These guys go from being blocked by the crowd to being up on the housetop, breaking through the roof to get their friend the help he required. Successful friendships help each other break through the barriers that life throws in our path. Displaying the conviction to act on your behalf to give you or get you the help you need when you need it is the hallmark of true friendship.

I love this story about the paralytic man because when his friends assist him, they amaze me by what they did *not* do as much as by what they did do.

    a. There is no record of a discussion or argument regarding the process of how they were going to get the paralytic man up on the roof. They did not let the process overshadow the goal. At times, the argument about how to help can be so disruptive to the process that the task is left undone.

    b. There is no record of the paralytic man

being more damaged as a result of the efforts of his friends. They did not get to the roof only to find, in the midst of all their activity, they had accidentally dropped their paralytic friend into the backyard. It is easy to get so caught up in the work of the work that we lose focus on the reason we are doing the work in the first place. A friend's help should not leave a person worse off than before help arrived.

c. They did not remind their friend throughout the process of how much they had done for him. They did not constantly parade the fact that they were making a sacrifice in his face like a big IOU to be collected. They did not attempt to make the friend feel as if he were now indebted for life to repay this act of kindness. No, his friends were not like that. His friends were conscientious in their convictions, and the results show the fruits of their collective efforts. They did not let station, status, or pride overcome the good deed needing to be done.

These four men showed compassion and conviction, put their paralytic friend on a pallet, carried him to Peter's house on their backs, lifted him onto the roof, and literally broke through the obstacles that hindered their paralytic friend from being made whole.

Does your level of conviction for your friends allow you to make sacrifices for their success, or are you just praying for them rather than being the answer to the prayer because sideline service is more convenient than getting in the game? All I know is that the story indicated that Jesus marveled at the compassion, commitment, and conviction of these men, and because of their faith on behalf of their friend, he made him whole. Success!

LIFE'S MISSING INGREDIENT—REAL FRIENDSHIP

A missing ingredient in the lives of many who will read this book is successful friendship. Successful friendship is enabling, not disabling. Successful friendship challenges and cultivates your character rather than corrupting it or condoning the lack thereof. Successful friendship engages in the types of dialogue that enrich, edify, and empower one another, not demean, disgrace, or defeat one another.

I have been around long enough to see my share of dysfunctional groups and individuals who considered themselves to be friends but lacked the essential elements needed to make one another whole. Friendships that are egocentric, lacking the ability to exchange honest feedback or criticism for fear of rejection or being considered disloyal, are friendships you can do without. Friendships that are predicated upon you subjecting your character or integrity to be part of the club or clique represent relationships that subtract from you and, in some cases, cripple you.

Friendships that are only functional when you are on the upside of life are the friendships similar to the ones the prodigal son made on his way to the pigpen of life. Those are the type of friends who will always be there for the party but will gossip about you and will not help you in your time of need. If your current friendships are draining life from you as opposed to refreshing and restoring you, and you are always the giver and never the recipient, I suggest you reevaluate your current friends.

The sacrifice of friendship is a noble offering not to be wasted on the trifling or the leech, for in the day of adversity a fake friend will abandon you. A key attribute in developing successful friendships is developing the ability to discern the difference.

Greater love has no man than this that he lay down his life for a friend. Successful friendship is the type that can bring a man from brokenness to wholeness. That type of successful friendship is better than chicken soup. It is essential to the soul!

Resource Utilization

Finances

> "Question: Are there any robbers in the house?"
> *Minister Rosa Centry*

This question, "Are there any robbers in the house?" is the hallmark question posed by my good friend and ministerial colleague Minister Rosa Centry. The question, however, is not original to her. God posed an interesting question to a friend of mine named Malachi. God asked a simple but subtle question, "Will a man rob God?" I have come to a remarkable conclusion; the answer is yes!

If you truly desire to live *life in the key of G*, you must master this chapter's concepts. There are four key concepts upon which you can literally transform your life forever. Financial freedom, and, ultimately, financial excellence, is teachings established on the interdependence of four key principles:

- Ownership

- Stewardship
- Giving
- Worship

Ownership

I equate understanding this concept of ownership to the part on the television show *Extreme Makeover* where they bring the family home, and everybody is waiting with tiptoe anticipation to show them the new house replacing the old one they left behind. However, before they can experience the new house, first they must "move that bus!"

It is the same process when it comes to our thinking about our finances. We must literally move the thing that blocks us from seeing and receiving that which God has prepared for us. That blockage is in our perceptions about ownership. I believe in order for a person to achieve excellence, he or she must develop holistically. In order for growth to occur spiritually, physically, emotionally, mentally, or financially, we must acknowledge God's authority. They must see their relationship with God as having relevance in every area of their lives.

If we do not feel or believe that God has a say in every area of our lives, we rebel against his authority and assert our own. This results in a subtle arrogance that convinces us we can compartmentalize areas in our life, putting boundaries or barriers around those areas we decide we can handle without God's input. It is my assertion that finances are one of the two primary areas in our lives where we decide we know more than God. (The second area is relationships.) If your finances are an area that you have decided that you can handle, God and the successful man or woman beg to differ. I hear you arguing already, so humor me and keep reading.

In college, the curriculum is formulated in a manner that encompasses a variety of disciplines in order that your capacity for learning is expanded. This desired expansion, however, might include courses that provide more challenge than we bargained for. We could often avoid these classes by dropping the course, by waiting for an easier teacher to come along, or by taking it in an environment where the academic rigor was reduced in order to more easily pass the class. But in order to complete a particular course of study and gain a degree in a particular subject matter, there were always a handful of courses that were required. They are called prerequisites or core courses.

You could try and cherry-pick your way through the curriculum to avoid those courses, but sooner or later the time would come when the piper had to be paid. These required courses ensure that certain information needed to master the essential aspects of the subject matter is acquired. If you failed to master this information, your learning experience would be viewed as incomplete and you could not go to the next level.

The same is true for mastering the concept of ownership. In fact, let's call the course Ownership 101. Whether you like it or not, know this: God owns everything. He is crystal clear on this fact and presents his ownership deed and title when he asserts, "The earth is the Lord's and all the fullness thereof, the world and those that dwell therein" (Psalm 24:1, NKJV). Yes, that means he owns all the stuff that you have told everyone else belongs to you. He not only owns your stuff, but he owns their stuff too. And if that were not enough, he owns you too! Once we understand that nothing we have belongs to us, then we can transition from the old mind-set of the arrogant owner and take on the appropriate role of the faithful steward.

Stewardship

Stewardship is the next aspect of this course that must be addressed. Stewardship equals accountability. Since we now know that what we have is on loan, it makes us accountable to use the resources provided in a manner consistent with the true owner's wishes and not our own. The true owner has asked for some unique things to be done with the income we receive. He gives us 100 percent and asks for the firstfruits of all our increase. Now, the term "firstfruits" may be a new one, so let me break it down for you. It means taking 10 percent off the top on all we earn and giving it to God. This is not a bad arrangement, especially when you consider that it all belongs to God, and he did not have to cut us in at all! This leads back to the earlier question: Will a man rob God? The answer is yes. But it raises a second question: Why? Consider this.

If I met you on the street and offered to give you one hundred dollars if, in return, you would give me back ten dollars, you would take that deal every time. Why, then, is it so hard to be accountable and give God what he requires? Why would you put the ninety dollars at risk by stealing the ten dollars? Maybe it is because you did not realize that when you give God the 10 percent, he automatically protects the 90 percent for you. This is what God told Malachi to tell his congregation in Malachi 3:11, but it gets even better than that. Can I share a recent revelation God gave me?

I was at my church, First Calvary Baptist Church, and Pastor Fredrick Amos Davis was gracious enough to give me some time in the morning services to illustrate a stewardship concept to the congregation. It began with a simple question: What do a grapefruit, an orange, an apple, and a dollar have in common? I proceeded with the help of Deacon Bobby Martin and resident fruit expert extraordinaire, Deacon Fred Jones (he's from Florida, and he never lets me forget that during football and basketball season) to cut open the fruit. Guess what was on the inside of the grapefruit, the apple, and the orange? *Seeds!* But I hear you again asking good questions: "What does that have to do with the dollar?" Stay with me.

If you plant a grapefruit seed, you reap a tree; not just any tree, but a grapefruit tree on which will grow many grapefruit. This is a fact confirmed by Fred Jones. It was originally established by God on the third day of creation when he said that every tree would yield fruit whose seed was in itself, after its kind. Now, when you plant an apple seed, guess what you reap? An apple tree! And when you plant the orange seed, you reap an orange tree! So still you ask, "What does that have to do with the dollar?"

Well, as people entered the sanctuary, I had the ushers give them each a dime. Now, don't sleep on this universal stewardship principle. The dimes I passed out to the congregation represented the seed contained in each dollar that God has commanded us to plant as a tithe in the fertile ground of God's storehouse. When we are obedient, we reap a harvest consistent with that of the seed planted. God said, "Test me in this, and see if I will not throw open the floodgates of heaven and pour out so much blessing that you will not have room enough for it" (Malachi 3:10, NIV). When you give God what he requires, he will give you what you desire!

Try it...I dare you.

Giving and Worship

The cold, hard facts are these: Giving and worship are directly connected. What you give to God is a direct reflection of what you think about God!

Giving is an action that is promoted out of an attitude of gratitude. The act cannot be successfully completed without the proper attitude. It is confirmed in scripture that worship is an activity born out of our affection toward God. Singing, shouting, expressing gladness, and giving thanks—all these actions are the direct result of the appreciation you feel toward God. I submit that it is difficult both to worship and to give to a God you feel disconnected from. But I also submit to you, if you are feeling disconnected from God, it is because of a breach in the relationship caused by you, not him. This testimony about God is true, even if our worship services have made it sound trite. God is good all the time, and all the time God is good.

This is the mind-set of the church of Macedonia in

2 Corinthians 8 who gave liberally unto Paul to support the work and expansion of the early church. They are remembered because they gave, not out of obligation but out of a willing heart, despite facing adverse economic circumstances. This giving was equated with their love for God. How's your giving stack up? Does it vary based upon circumstances? Is your giving a true and accurate reflection of your love for God? Worship is not a selfish activity. Neither is giving.

In 1 Chronicles 29, David knew this, and he gave heavily to fund the church that his son Solomon would build. This act of worship set in motion a level of giving from the leadership and people. So powerful was this outpouring by the people that it caused David to ask God how the people could give so. A portion of David's prayer in verse 14, "All things comes of Thee, O Lord and of thine own have we given thee," is an anthem sung after the offering in churches all over our country. The acknowledgment of who owns what is pivotal to having a proper perspective on giving and worship. Your testimony of trust in God through giving offers an empowering testimony to others. It offers encouragement when you share how God has moved in your life. As a result, others will experience, some for the first time, the freedom of worshipping the God who gives stuff rather than worshipping the stuff that God gives.

Giving requires us to act on what we say we know about ownership and stewardship. What we have belongs to God, and we are accountable to make sure that what is required by him is given. Yet the tithe, however, continues to be a thorn in the side of many Christians. The cold, hard facts are these: If you struggle to give to God, two situations may be true:

a. You don't trust God

b. You don't really love God

There has been much struggle over this simple biblical concept. You can reference back as far as Cain and Abel, and tithing has been an issue. The term "worship" conveys with it the idea of worth. In other words, what you give God directly expresses to God what you think he is worth. If you steal his tithe after he has blessed you in abundance, you send him a clear but negative worth statement. Maybe this illustration will bring it home for you.

If your spouse tells you he or she loves you but decides to share his or her intimacy with another, this would be problematic. Why? Because trust has been broken and that which has been ordained through the covenant of marriage to be reserved for you has been shared with some other party. It will be difficult for your spouse, despite his or her excuses, apologies, and declarations of love, to convince you of his or her love because he or she has violated your trust. Let's take it to the bridge. When you take that which should have been set apart for God and spend it at Nordstrom's, Neiman Marcus, Macy's, the club, or for golf, vacation, time-shares, Christmas, Mother's Day, or Easter outfits, you commit adultery and break trust with God!

He gave you 100 percent and can't trust you to give

him back 10 percent? Then, when your finances get funny and your change is strange and your month outlasts your money, you have the audacity to ask why or ask for more? In fact, I had this thought that could solve tithing for good. See, God loves you so much and would hate for you to be found out as a liar, so what if he did this?

What if God accumulates your giving for the past year and takes whatever you give as tithes (i.e., the 10 percent) and adjusts your income (i.e., the 100 percent) to line up with your tithes? For example, if you make $100,000 and you give fifty dollars a week as your tithes, God should adjust your gross income to $26,000 to match the tithes given since fifty dollars x fifty-two weeks equals $2,600 instead of the $10,000 you should have cheerfully given.

What do you mean, "That's not fair"? It is as fair as you robbing God and lying to him week in and week out by submitting a tithe envelope that is a fraud. The good thing about God is that he is good and his mercy truly endures forever, but what a thought.

Elements of Good Stewardship

Now let's talk about the 90 percent God leaves under your control. How well are you handling what God allows you to keep? If you are living paycheck to paycheck, if your money is funny, your change is strange, and you are tithing, we need to handle a few additional aspects of stewardship. Here are several quick recommendations to help you.

Budgeting

A key instrument in becoming accountable as a steward is to be disciplined about how you handle the resources with which God has entrusted you. A budget is a tool that serves to organize your financial resources so that you see where you are and provides a road map to help you get where you need to be. You don't want your financial life to be like the children of Israel that wandered for forty years in circles when they were literally right across the street from the Promised Land. A budget is the road map to keep you from being financially lost.

Saving

A key component to the budget must be setting aside a portion of your earnings for yourself. Saving is a lost art in this credit-crazed society. It is recommended from most financial advisors that after tithes, the next action should be to pay yourself, even before bills and other obligations. Some recommend that you make that payment 10 percent as well. I say start off with a minimum of 5 percent and increase it as you pay off debts. Your budget should then address the remaining 80 to 85 percent of income you take home.

Investments

You should start investing a portion of your money in investment vehicles that will create wealth over the long haul. You should get reputable assistance from those who know what they are doing (i.e., licensed professionals with reputable firms). I want to highlight the low-hanging fruit that investment in a 401(k) represents. A 401(k) is an investment with one of the highest returns because of the employer-matching component, which is free money. Most plans match your contributions at some percentage up to a predetermined threshold. For instance, if you save a portion your salary via the 401(k) and your employer matches the first 6 percent with a 50 percent match, you should set aside that 6 percent at minimum to get the additional 3 percent match. Fifty percent is a return on investment you cannot afford to pass up!

Wealth Protection and Preservation

Please use a reputable financial planner you trust as part of your team that helps you to set wise investment goals and make informed investment decisions. Part of that advice must be that you create a will. This is nonnegotiable! It makes no sense to amass savings and not take advantage of the tax benefits related to wealth transfer or, worse, allow the state to make those decisions for you at a significant cost to your estate and your loved ones. Now if you love the state, ignore everything I've said, do nothing, and just give them your money! Don't neglect your responsibility as good steward to protect the inheritance that you are leaving to your children's children. It is a poor testimony to have no will, no financial plan, no savings, no insurance, and no idea of how your children will be cared for in the event of your death or disability. I recently sat in a conference of executives as the subject of wealth management was discussed, and even among informed, financially literate, business-savvy individuals, the consistent theme was that there was great room for improvement. No matter whether you have modest or mega means, the responsibility to manage the resources that have been entrusted to you is important.

In fact, good stewardship was so important that Jesus told a parable recorded in Matthew 25 of the men who had been given talents to manage. One was given five, one was given two, and the other one. When the investor returned from the first man who he gave five talents, he received ten. From the man whom he had given two talents, he received four. But from the man whom he had given one talent, he received excuses about why he had hidden the talent as opposed to investing it more wisely. Many of you are asking for more when, if truth were told, you have not done a good job with the resources entrusted to you to date.

So look at where you are; assess the state of affairs. Where you have done well, congratulations. Where you see need for improvement, make a plan and take action. Remember, stewardship equals accountability. The better your accountability, the greater your stewardship.

In Case I Made You Mad...

Take a ticket and stand in line. You will not be the first or the last when it comes to this subject. Money is one of the toughest subjects to confront an individual on, especially if this is not an area that you have submitted to God's authority. If you won't submit to his authority, I certainly can't force you to submit to my humble request. But at the risk of pushing the envelope with your ego, anger, and arrogance, consider this: I hear your mind raising arguments, telling me you already know all the stuff I have shared and that you are fine. You certainly don't want to hear another person, especially a preacher, tell you what to do with your money.

If you say you know better financially, then my question is, why don't you do better? If you knew what you knew, how is it that you do what you do? My thought is that if you knew better, you would do better. The definition in some circles for a fool is someone who will continue to do the same thing expecting a different result. In my circles, the definition for foolishness is knowing the voice of God, rejecting his prescription for prosperity, and, as a result, placing all connected to them under God's disfavor. Remember this:

- Information with application leads to transformation

- Information without application leads to frustration

You choose.

Follow-Through

> "An essential difference between the people who dream great things versus the person that achieves great things is . . . Follow-through."
>
> *D. A. Gregory, Sr.*

If writing a book is any indication, finishing a task is much harder than starting one. In fact, I would hazard to hunch that all of us have a project or two outstanding on the portfolio of life's unfinished projects. For some, the parking lot of life is littered with "would haves," "could haves," and "should haves"—the residue of things started but never finished. In my personal pursuit of success, I have read several books and articles profiling the lives of successful people from all walks of life and have noted that a common trait they each seemed to possess is the ability to follow through.

Based on my research and conversations, a common reason given for the failure to achieve one's goals or objectives is the lack of discipline to finish what one started. If I have hit a sore point or if the issue of starting but not finishing is an area of personal struggle for you, then I hope this chapter serves as the catalyst to help you master the life-changing lesson of follow-through.

What Is Follow-Through?

Webster's Dictionary defines follow-through as the continuing of an action or task to its desired conclusion. My laymen's definition is succinct and to the point: finishing what you started. Both definitions sound simple enough. Why, then, is following through so hard? I am glad you asked! Maybe a discussion of some primary reasons for failure will help shed light on this mystery.

Reasons People Fail to Follow Through

Reason #1

Underpreparation–The Bible has an oft-quoted passage that uses a building illustration to make a point. The passage indicated that no one builds a building unless he or she first stops to count the cost! Many projects have ended in failure not because of a lack of energy or because the idea is not great or grand. These projects fail for a fundamental reason: the person failed to plan. A critical element in the success of any endeavor is the level of effort put into the planning process. An old proverb says, "If you fail at planning, you will succeed at failure."

Reason #2

Overconfidence–Another trait I observed in those who are successful is the trait of humility. It is a magnetic quality that attracts and enables others who are willing to contribute to your success. Overconfidence has the exact opposite function. Overconfidence is a repellant that operates much like OFF, the insect repellant. When one is overconfident and arrogant, it literally creates an aroma that turns people off, aborts or cuts off resources, and most of all puts off assistance. The uncanny reality is often the members of this annoyed group are often the very individuals who hold the resources and contacts critical to your success. This may result in people who possess the very help you need choosing instead to sit on the sidelines of life, watching with great excitement, awaiting your failure rather than assisting in your success.

Reason #3

Procrastination–The ugly twin sister to overconfidence is procrastination. Both are pride based. While the overconfident think too highly of themselves, the procrastinator assumes he or she has time to accomplish tomorrow what he or she could invest quality time and effort to complete today. The procrastinator is the one you inevitably see rushing at the last minute, trying to muscle a process, call in a favor, or obtain a hookup to accomplish the ordinary through extraordinary means. This approach tends to result in obvious procedural errors, blown deadlines, poor-quality workmanship, significant errors, omissions, and lost opportunities, all because they wasted the valuable commodity called time. Remember, the procrastinator makes a high-stakes bet that the window of opportunity will always be open when he or she chooses to go through it. And who knows, the window may be open when the procrastinator gets there, but, unfortunately, the room may be empty because opportunity left out the door on the other side of the room—with the prepared.

Reason # 4

Lack of research rather than resource—When you read this statement, do not shut me down by jumping to a false conclusion that I am financially well off or that I have access to unlimited resources. I do recognize, as do most of you, that it takes resources to accomplish almost anything you do. The reality for most of us is that we personally do not possess the needed resources to fund our dreams; neither do our friends, family, or close associates. So what do you have? I am glad you asked. The answer is research!

I had an interesting discussion with a friend of mine who introduced me to the world of private equity financing. I was explaining to Anita my dilemma related to several multimillion-dollar projects for which I was part of a group trying to obtain funding. She could tell that I was disconcerted because the level of financing to me was a big hurdle. She smiled and asked me what percentage of deals I thought she did where people had great ideas but less than an ideal amount of capital to invest.

I said 10 or 15 percent. She smiled again and indicated the greater majority of the deals, 80 to 90 percent, were undercapitalized. What Anita went on to explain to me was profound. She indicated that the strength of the deal for her was often in the level of research the potential candidate had done to demonstrate to her why this deal could make money for her investors. She wanted to know if I understood how the business would make its money. She proceeded to question me regarding the demographic, area competitors, and experience and background of the deal partners. As we got deeper into the projections and the details, it hit me. She was like my fifth-grade math teacher; all she really wanted to know is that I had done my homework. She already had the resources.

Anita represents people who have money but lack the ideas or projects that will make it grow. Her job is to take their funds and invest with or in people who have solid ideas that create opportunity to meet her clients' expectations regarding return on investment. She asked questions and wanted answers that demonstrated that I had done my due diligence. By doing my homework I was demonstrating that I had put in the appropriate level of effort to clearly articulate the vision, to demonstrate a full appreciation of the risks and challenges involved in the venture and the leadership skills to execute a plan that would create a win-win for both sides. If I had not done adequate research, they would clearly choose not to invest.

The moral of the story is many of us have ideas from time to time on how we want to achieve success, but when we pitch that idea to others, the more questions we are asked, the vaguer we become. This signals to the listener that you have not done your homework. This may be in the form of your business plan or some other road map that you are trying to use to convince others to buy into your idea. If you have not done your homework, it will show up. Success is the return on investment for the hard work of homework.

REASON #5

Lack of Discipline—Certain things are guaranteed in this life, and tough times are one of them. Inevitably, in the attempt to achieve any goal, tough times will come. As an audit and risk management consultant, I review financial operations, business and strategic planning documents, and internal controls. One of the critical facets or phases of my review is the risk assessment. I purposely pose what-if statements that address potential negative occurrences to determine if my client has identified and prepared to address certain risks, some that may be unavoidable based on that business or industry. My experience has proven that if they have thought through various scenarios and possible options prior to the problems occurring, they will respond much better when actually tested.

In his prime, Mike Tyson was the most feared presence in boxing. It was interesting to watch his opponents. Each of them had similarities:

- They all signed the contract to fight.
- They all participated in the prefight hype.
- They all had plans on how they would approach the fight.
- They all had plans to win.

Mike, however, had a reality check for their plans, the ultimate what-if scenario to test each fighter's plan; he was going to hit them! Mike had a very simple belief learned from Cus D'Amato, his first trainer: "Everybody has a plan until they get hit!" Mike understood that many had not truly planned for the adversity that comes with getting hit. Unfortunately, just as with Mike's opponents, once hit, we abandon the planning and the strategy we started with because we did not adequately plan for tough times.

In any good plan, we must always address the possibility that hard times will come. Planning for them requires discipline and gives you your plan of action so that you can be responsive rather than reactionary to the challenges that life may bring your way. Exhibiting the discipline to make a good plan will often allow you to be proactive in anticipating the obstacles that can prolong, postpone, or even prohibit your ability to follow through with your plans.

So What Are the Key Elements Involved in Follow-Through?

Do your homework—Much like our discussion regarding the importance of research, know where others have struggled or failed in trying to accomplish the same task. If you are attempting something that has never been done before, study other great people and the skills and traits that made them successful and pay attention to how they responded to failure.

Be resilient—It will likely not happen the way you dreamed it would happen. Joseph did not see the pit,

Potipher's house (slavery), and prison in his path to the palace that God initially showed him. The costs are normally higher; the road is normally longer; the challenges may come more frequent than waves on an angry sea. The negatives may outweigh the positives, and you see more reasons to stop than to continue, but keep failing, or, as noted author John Maxwell says, "failing forward." The greatest victories are often experienced after defeat.

Perform under pressure–In football, they refer to the area between the twenty-yard line and the goal line as the red zone. It is named such because it is a compressed space where the greatest contention takes place because it is the area of greatest value. It is a highly pressurized area where both the offense and the defense are forced to execute at their highest levels. If a defensive player loses his focus and misses an assignment, the opposing team's offense will score. If the offensive player becomes lax or loses concentration or forgets his play, the defensive player may be able to take advantage, causing a fumble or an interception, causing the offense not to score. With the game on the line, no matter whether on offense or defense, it is important that he perform under pressure. The same is true for you!

Practice like you want to play–So many desire to be game day stars, but stars are made in practice. No matter you level of natural, God-given ability, practice is where you hone your skills to be able to deliver during crunch time. Everyone is marveling at the unprecedented Olympic success of our newest superstar, my homeboy, Baltimore's own, Michael Phelps, who swam himself into the hearts and minds of America while making Olympic history.

Kids and adults were staying up late, surrounding the television just to see this young man achieve the unthinkable: eight gold medals in one Olympics! Unthinkable—certainly not! This is what Michael Phelps prepared for.

During the Olympics the press highlighted the training routine that Michael had to maintain just to get ready to swim. The practice routine seemed to be more grueling than the actual competition itself. But it is in practice, the times when no one is watching you, that you win the event. It is when it is just you, the coach, and your biggest opponent—yourself—that you make the decision to commit to do what it takes to achieve greatness. Game day success is only a reflection of prior practice and perseverance. It is the intersection of preparation and opportunity.

Why Is Follow-Through so Important?

I played baseball growing up in Baltimore, and I was fortunate to have as a coach Mr. Osceola Smith, affectionately known as Mr. Smitty. Mr. Smitty was a former Negro League baseball player who resided in the community of Turners Station and for some forty years taught countless young men how to play baseball. He had four simple rules that were not only rules for hitting a baseball; they were rules for living life. The first rule is:

- *Stay low*—In baseball, the setup for how you address the ball is very important. If you stand too erect or you are too crouched, it would be more difficult to hit the ball because you would be off balance. Life is similar; if you think too highly of yourself or have low self-esteem, you will not address life successfully.

The second rule is:

- *Keep focused*–Mr. Smitty said, "If you see the ball, you just might hit the ball." On the baseball field, there are many distractions—players moving, coaches signaling, the catcher and pitcher exchanging signs, your mama hollerin' in the stands, and with all that going on, as a batter, you only have one objective—hit the ball! Life is similar. It is filled with distractions—family pressures, peer pressures, internal and external expectations, yet you must block all that out to make the right decisions that will keep you focused on what you are supposed to be doing. Make solid contact and hit the ball. Batter up!

The third rule is:

- *Swing hard*–Mr. Smitty let us know, as only your coach can, that you are in the batter's box to hit the ball, and to hit the ball you must swing the bat! And since you have a bat, you might as well swing hard! Swing hard is metaphorical for putting forth your best effort. To this day, nothing irritates me more than to watch a player get called out on strikes without swinging the bat. He or she struck out just looking. You were not put in the batter's box just to look! You were put there to swing, and if you are going to swing, swing hard! Putting forth your best effort is a discipline we must master if we are to be successful in any endeavor in life. I consider it to be a prerequisite for success.

Mr. Smitty's fourth and final rule, and arguably the most important, is:

- *Follow through*—I watched Josh Hamilton's record-breaking performance during the Major League's All-Star Home Run Derby—twenty-eight home runs in one round. His swing, fundamentally sound, was a sight to behold not only for the fundamentals but also because of his follow-through! Young players often stop their swing because they are so excited (or surprised) to have made contact with the ball. As a result of aborting their swing, the ball does not go very far. Mr. Smitty taught us to swing the bat, critiquing our form, so that we could get the maximum out of our efforts.

The fact is, what Mr. Smitty taught us is universal in its application. Whether you are:

- Barry Bonds hitting a home run,
- Tiger Woods crushing a drive or sinking a fifty-foot birdie putt,

- Dwayne Wade or Kobe dropping a game-winning twenty footer,

- Venus or Serena exchanging blistering serves and ground strokes at Wimbledon, or

- Henri kicking a breakaway goal to win a World Cup championship,

all require follow-through.

It is the power of follow-through that propels the ball over the fence, in the basket, over the net, or in the goal.

The same is true for life. Anything your desire to do academically, entrepreneurially, professionally, even spiritually, requires follow-through to reach success. The faith to follow through is the differentiating and distinguishing characteristic between those who don't and those who do. Which one are you?

Don't Quit

Anonymous

When things go wrong, as they sometimes will,
When the road you're trudging seems all uphill,
When the funds are low and the debts are high,
And you want to smile, but you have to sigh,
When care is pressing you down a bit,
Rest if you must; but don't you quit.

Life is queer with its twists and turns,
As everyone of us sometimes learns,
And many a failure turns about
When he might have won had he stuck it out;
Don't give up, though the pace seems slow;
You might succeed with another blow.

Often the goal is nearer than
It seems to a faint and faltering man,
Often the struggler has given up
When he might have captured the victor's cup.
And he learned too late, when the night slipped down,
How close he was to the golden crown.

Success is failure turned inside out;
The silver tint of the clouds of doubt;
And you never can tell how close you are,
It may be near when it seems afar;
So stick to the fight when you're hardest hit;
It's when things seem worst that you mustn't quit.

Divine Participation

Favor

> "It has been said that favor ain't fair but it's the way I know that God is there!"
>
> *D. A. Gregory, Sr.*

I am so glad that you did not quit and stuck it out to get to this point. The seven preceding chapters were meant to help you lay the foundation for living *life in the key of G*. The first three chapters highlighted our focus, faith, and fellowship. These chapters were designed to address the vertical integration—the relationship each of us needs to have with God.

The next two chapters dealt with family and friends. These chapters highlighted our horizontal orientation and spoke to the primary and fundamental aspects of relationships that we have with our fellow man. These relationships often get marred or messed up because they are directly tied to the intensity and consistency of the vertical relationship we maintain with God.

The succeeding two chapters were probably the longest in the book, but they focused on critical battlegrounds consistently highlighted as areas of greatest struggle: finance and follow-through. The effective utilization of our talent is intimately tied to our stewardship over both our most valuable resources: time and our treasure. Finances can often become the graveyard for our dreams and desires because of wrong beliefs, poor stewardship, and generational money mismanagement inherited from our parents or learned from our peers. Follow-through can either be the catalyst, the intersection where our faith and our works come together into meaningful actions to make our dreams a reality, or the lack of follow-through can create the coffin where our dreams go to die. Many times just having a good understanding and making proper and consistent application of the principles in the first seven chapters will result in the desired outcomes, thus providing the success we are looking for.

However, this chapter is special. It is reserved for that someone who is reading this book who has special dreams that are far bigger than your abilities. You have been faithful in applying the principles yet still have not achieved your goal. There you sit, broken down on the road of life, trying to sense out of your situation while others pass you by.

I have been sent to share with you that there will be occasions when you have done all that you know how to do, your absolute best, yet more is required. I have searched the scriptures and even looked into my own life experience and recognized situations where there was a gap. A gap! What do you mean a gap?

You know, a gap:

- A distance between what you have and what you need
- A shortfall between your dream and your reality
- A gap between what God had shown you in your heart and convinced you that he wants you to do and what you actually see

Don't faint; the gap was meant to be. The truth of the matter is, God specializes in creating expectations and experiences that seem to be in conflict for the express purpose of bridging this so-called gap. How does he bridge this gap? By giving you his favor. What is favor? Glad you asked. Favor is God's anointed presence (i.e., g.a.p.). He specializes in making his will for our lives come to pass in the most adventurous and unexpected manner, always leaving this *gap* that only he can fill for our good and for his glory. I call this "Divine Participation."

To claim to fully understand how this process works would be to tell a lie. For I still, like you, see through the glass dimly, often struggling to make sense of his will and heads or tails of his ways. But I have picked up a couple of points along the way that may serve to alleviate your frustration while you come to accept his sovereignty as he does things with your life to bring about his perfect will. That's my nice way of telling you suck it up 'cause God is more interested in you conforming to his will than your convenience in the process. Let's go!

Favor–It Has an Order

There is a fact, a universal truth, regarding favor. It is a nonnegotiable reality that so many of us fail to discern and often overlook. There is an order to obtaining favor. Jesus himself demonstrated it in his youth and modeled it in his actions throughout his short but power-packed stay on Earth. Luke, in his gospel account, records this powerful prescription for living, noting "that Jesus increased in wisdom and stature and in favor with God and man" (Luke 2:52, NKJV). Did you miss it? Notice the order: God and man.

In this status-conscious culture of networking name-droppers and professional powerbrokers, we tend to be more concerned with currying the favor of the politically or professionally connected. Jesus' example, however, suggests a more excellent way. Luke seemingly implies by this order an intentional preference that would suggest seeking God's favor over man's as the more advantageous route to true success. Why is that? I am glad you asked, but I would have told you anyway. Let's look a little closer at our text, for the gospel historian Luke references an attribute of supreme importance to understanding and obtaining favor that we should consider.

The text stated that Jesus grew in wisdom. I cannot overemphasize the importance of this point. In a society that is quick to recognize any and every other choice but God, having the wisdom to put God first gives you an awesome and anointed advantage. Wisdom will take you where book smarts, street savvy, whom you know, and what you know can't go. You may be more qualified, more degreed, more well known, more accomplished, and you will still get passed by on the highway of opportunity by the man or woman who has God's favor.

Solomon, the wise king, dedicated the entire eighth chapter of Proverbs to describing the benefits of wisdom but brings it home in verse 35. Solomon said, "He who finds me (wisdom) finds life and obtains favor from the Lord." Jesus states the same principle a different way, but the essence remains the same. Jesus said, "But seek ye first the kingdom of God and his righteousness and all these other things will be added unto you (Matthew 6:33, NKJV). So let's recap to be sure we are clear. If you have the wisdom to seek God first, you will find *life* and God's favor. Sounds simple.

Favor—It Is Unique in Its Operation

As simple as our earlier conclusion may sound, the circumstances of life are anything but. God seems to specialize in operating outside our comfort zone and will allow or provide circumstances where only he and his divine favor can produce the desired results. The scriptures overflow with examples of men and women who were challenged by God to exercise a level of faith that moved beyond their capabilities. This is an uncomfortable place for those who may have enjoyed a modicum of success doing things "my way." Living *life in the key of G* will inevitably result in God creating or allowing situations that eclipse all that we are so he can be all that we need. For example:

- Abraham was to get out of his country, away

from his family, and out of his father's house to go to a land he would show him. Try taking that message home to the wife. I hear the wheels of your mind turning. Couldn't he make Abraham great right where he was? After all, he is God, isn't he? He could have, but he didn't. Keep reading.

- Joseph had a dream that one day he would be a ruler and even his father and brothers would bow to him. But the dream did not disclose the nightmare of his brothers' brutality and the experience of being thrown in a pit, sold into slavery, and later prison as the preparatory path to a palace existence!

- Moses was told to go back to Egypt, the place of his princely upbringing, the place he was fugitive from, to tell Pharaoh, "Let my people go." Why not use a king from a neighboring country, somebody with an army? And if that were not enough, God, once Pharaoh agrees to let the people go, purposely leads them out of Egypt into a natural cul-de-sac—mountains, desert, and, oh yeah, the Red Sea. And to put the cherry on top, God makes Pharaoh change his mind about letting the people go.

- Joshua was commissioned to lead the descendants of a rebellious congregation of complainers who had spent the last forty years wandering in a circle to occupy a promised land where eviction notices had not been served to the current residents.

- Simon (Peter), tired after fishing all night long and catching nothing, was nice enough to let a young preacher friend of his brother use his boat as a sermon pulpit to preach to the masses. This young preacher, after finishing his sermon, imposes further by making another request: "Launch out into the deep and let down your nets for a catch.

Each of you knows the biblical stories highlighted, but the one that irritated me the most was the story of Joseph. As I read the story about all he had to endure, the author kept interjecting that the LORD was with Joseph! In the pit? In slavery at Potipher's house? In prison? Where? Where was God?

In the midst of the most troubling aspects of our lives, we all sometimes ask these questions:

- Why me, God?

- Why is he doing this to me or allowing this to happen in my life? I'm serving him, trying to live for him, trying to do what I thought he told me to do. I'm on his side, but I ain't feelin' him right now in the midst of these trials and tribulations.

- What's up, God?

- Where are you?

But in the midst of my questioning, God spoke to me

and told me ever so softly that "favor is not the absence of adversity; it is the presence of God." Having God's favor does not mean you will not have issues; it just means that your issues will not have you.

- You may have to separate from family, friends, and the familiarity of your comfort zone.
- Abraham told me, "You may have to leave a *Lot* behind."
- You may have to suffer a significant reversal of fortune or personal ridicule.
- You may even appear to have taken what everyone around you will consider a loss.

Yes, weeping may endure for a night, but hold on, for joy does come in the morning! Adversity is no more than the stagehands of life working to construct the setting for God to manifest a miracle for your good and his glory. This, however, requires us to activate another key attribute.

Favor—It Requires Obedience

Obedience is an essential attribute that must be exercised to receive God's favor. Oftentimes the situations constructed are no more than tests to determine if God can trust you with the level of blessing with which he desires to entrust you. Saul, the first king of Israel, lost it all because he could not follow directions. David's deathbed commission to his son, Solomon, was to obey the commands of God. In his commissioning service for Joshua, Moses' protégé, God gives the secret of true prosperity, telling Joshua to speak the Word, meditate on the Word day and night, and do all that the Word says do, for then you shall make your way prosperous and you shall have good success!

There is a trust that is exhibited by those who are credited with having God's favor and marked by the ability to obey his commands even when they did not understand why or if things were going to work out. There, there, I see I have hit a nerve because you believe you have to understand. You believe that you have to be "in the know" or have some guarantee before you can trust. You feel like God should provide you a script like some B-movie actor who needs his or her lines to perform. This ain't that type of party.

Your obedience to God is not contingent upon your understanding anything. His ways are not your ways, neither are your thoughts his thoughts. God's program is not subject to your sign-off. He is the potter, and you are the clay. Your service is without qualification or precondition. It requires a level of trust that does not compromise in the face of adversity.

- It is a trust that allows Daniel to face sure death in the lions' den for continuing his ritual of prayer.

- It is a trust that kept three Hebrew boys sentenced to death in a fiery furnace from bowing down to a golden idol.

- It is a trust that, despite more bad news in one day than anyone should receive in a lifetime, allowed Job to declare in the midst of his trials, "Though he slay me, yet will I trust him" (Job 13:15, NKJV).

- It is the type of faith that allows a widow woman at the brink of bankruptcy and family displacement to go door to door, borrowing pots, knowing she has nothing to put in them because the prophet Elisha said to.

And it is this type of trust that underscores the true mark of favor, which is the ability to overcome.

Favor—The Ability to Overcome

The hallmark of a Christian is the ability to overcome and to prosper. Jesus promised us that in this life we would experience trials and tribulation, but he encouraged us to be of good cheer, for he has overcome the world. This overcoming power is part of our inheritance that each of us as Christians has access to if we trust and obey. This prescription is as tried and true as my grandmother's yeast rolls recipe. If you follow the instructions, you will experience a result that will be satisfying to your soul. Please don't take my word for it; try God for yourself and join the long legacy of believers past and present who can testify to his gap-filling grace, mercy, and supernatural providence on their behalf. He will not only meet your needs, but he has a track record of exceeding our wildest expectations. Check the record; look at the list

Abraham—He believed, he obeyed, and he fathered

Isaac and became the father of many nations and the beginning of the lineage through which Jesus would come.

Joseph–He believed, he obeyed, remaining steadfast from the pit to the palace, saving Egypt and his family from the famine, and he became the prince of Egypt.

Moses–He believed, he obeyed, and with a rod that represented the presence, power, and provision of God, he divided the Red Sea, crossed over on dry land, and led the children of Israel out of slavery in Egypt.

Joshua–He believed, he obeyed, picking up the mantle of Moses, and he led the children of Israel into the Promised Land, conquering all that dared to oppose. He even asked God to make the sun stand still to finish the defeat of his enemies, and it was granted.

Daniel–He believed, he obeyed, surviving the lion's den without a scratch, proving prayer changes things.

Shadrach, Meshach, and Abednego–They believed, they obeyed, and they danced and praised God in the fire with only their bonds being consumed and exited the fire unhurt, with not even the smell of smoke in their garments.

Job–He believed, he obeyed, and he received double for his trouble. He had more sons and daughters, greater possessions, a longer life, and greater respect from his friends and his enemy, the devil.

The Widow Woman–She believed, she obeyed the man of God's instructions and borrowed the pots from her neighbors and miraculously filled every pot from the little cruse of oil that she had. She was able to pay her husband's debts and save her sons from slavery all because she trusted and obeyed.

Each of our biblical references has a consistent thread to his or her testimony. They trusted and obeyed God and overcame the obstacles because of the miraculous presence and favor of God. But I would be remiss if I did not end with whom I began the chapter.

Jesus grew in wisdom and stature. Let this mind be in you that was also in Christ Jesus, for Jesus believed and obeyed God's plan to come down through forty and two generations and disrobe himself of glory and in humility clothe himself in human flesh, taking on the form of a man. He was obedient, even to the point of death on a cross! Now, to the world it would appear that he had taken the ultimate *L*. His disciples, save John, had deserted him. His mama, family, and friends in his calling circle were left disconnected, and then the unthinkable happened—he died. They took his lifeless body and placed Jesus in a borrowed tomb, rolled a huge stone over the entrance, and placed a Roman guard to ensure no one could steal the body. The fat lady had been delivered her sheet music and had rehearsed her song and was on stage at the mic. It was a wrap. But do you remember what I told you? The unmistakable mark of favor is the ability to overcome!

And early Sunday morning, Jesus got up and snatched the keys from hell, broke death's stinger, blasted a hole in the grave's bottom, and put boots to Satan, stomping him so hard he bruised his heel. He stepped up on resurrection ground, snatching the sheet music from the fat lady's stand, put her off stage, and then made his own announcement: "All power in heaven and in earth is given unto me!" Therefore, he has been given a name that is above every name. At the name of Jesus, every knee must bow and every tongue must confess that Jesus Christ is Lord to the glory of God. What does this mean to you and me, you might ask? It means everything!

The favor of God is not found in club nor clique or in sorority nor fraternity. It is not a privilege reserved for the country club member. It is available to king or peasant, master or servant. The one who ordains favor is no respecter of person. He is not impressed by your status, station, affluence, or affiliation. He is available to those who trust and obey. He is available to you.

Favor is God's almighty presence bridging the gap so that you might experience the life that he promised you could have. Even when it looks like you have or are about to take a loss, he is able to do exceedingly, abundantly above all you ask or think, according to the power that works in us. That power is fueled by a faith to believe that he can do just what he has said—a faith that allows us to act like a thing is so, even when it's not so, in order that it might be so. Jesus said, "That the thief comes to steal, kill and destroy," and we know this to be true. All of us have experienced the hurtful pains that sin and Satan cause in our lives, but Jesus did not stop there. He continued by saying, "I have come that they might have life and that they may have it more abundantly" (John 10:10, NKJV). Many of us have believed him and have received life, but he promised more! And I want you to believe him for more!

I believe in the power of God, and I want you to believe in his power to give you his favor, that you may experience an exceptional life here on this side of heaven. There is more to life than you are experiencing right now. There is life on the other side of the comma, and it is called abundant life. Since he promised that I could have it, I want it. What about you? I know what God has for me; it is for me, and the same is true for your life!

- Believe him for your life,
- Trust him with your life,
- Worship him in your life,

I guarantee your life will be filled with God's anointed presence—his favor, the unmistakable mark of one living *life in the key of G*!

Epilogue

If you are reading this, congratulations! You finished the book. Thank you for your time and your vote of confidence to add this resource to your library. It is my hope that you have richly benefited from the subjects covered in this book and will continue to reap the harvest throughout your life as you put these principles to work in your life.

The vertical integration chapters covering focus, faith, and fellowship deal with understanding and aligning your life with God's purpose for your life. To know what God wants from you requires you to spend time with God, talking with him, and, more importantly, listening to him. The time spent improving your vertical integration with God has a natural carryover effect into your horizontal orientation, improving relationships with family and friends (and even enemies). The improvement both these areas facilitate is the ability to improve your resource utilization. Your usage of your time, talent, and treasure in his service is integral to living a successful life.

Our frustration often comes when we exhibit a lack of discipline in our stewardship over these resources.

The wonderful part of this adventure that I hope you experience is the unmatched feeling when God bridges the gap in your life to make your dreams a reality and even brings victory out of defeat. I hope you experience his loving favor as he brings about a significant reversal of fortune through his divine participation to work things out for your good and for his glory.

As I noted earlier, living *life in the key of G* is simply living life according to the manufacturer's blueprint. If we utilize his instruction manual and participate in routine conference calls and follow his directions, we can have the guarantee that God gave Joshua in his commissioning service as the new leader of the children of Israel. If you observe his Word and do his will, you will make your way prosperous, and you will have good success. That's how we live *life in the key of G*.

Unlock Your Life

I would be remiss if I ended this book without ensuring that you have the one element required to live *life in the key of G*. You need a relationship with God. The only way this relationship can be achieved is through salvation. Jesus said in John 15:5 (NKJV), "I am the vine and we are the branches... and without him we can do nothing." It is for that reason that God so loved the world that "He gave His only begotten Son, that whoever believes in Him should not perish but have everlasting life (John 3:16, NKJV). If you want that life, pray this prayer:

Heavenly Father, I come to you admitting that I am a sinner. I desire today to turn away from my sin, and I ask you to cleanse me from my old ways. I believe that your son, Jesus, died on the cross for my sins. I also believe that he arose from the dead, and through my belief in him I would be forgiven of my sins and be made righteous through his sacrifice for me. I declare, by faith in the name of Jesus the Christ, my freedom from sin and ask that you fill me with the power of the Holy Spirit. Thank you, LORD, for saving me.

If you prayed this prayer, you are on your way to living *life in the key of G*. Go and be great in God. Drop me an e-mail at www.aftercross.com so we can join in the celebration.

Be blessed!

About the Author

Derric A. Gregory, Sr. is the President of Dimension Partners LLC and serves as an Associate Minister at the First Calvary Baptist Church in Durham, NC. A dynamic author, preacher, and teacher of God's Word, Derric now steps out of the wings to provide this provocative yet practical literary offering.

Derric is a gifted leader, an accomplished business executive, and has been a licensed certified public accountant for over twenty years, developing a blue-chip corporate pedigree that uniquely qualifies him to bridge between the spiritual and secular arenas. He is member of the Executive Leadership Council, the National Association of Black Accountants, Inc., the American Institute of Certified Public Accountants, and the National Association of Corporate Directors. He serves on the boards of Meharry Medical College and the Foundation Board of North Carolina Central University. He is a Summa Cum Laude graduate of North Carolina A&T State University and is an active member of the star-studded Beta Phi chapter of Omega Psi Phi Fraternity,

Inc. His greatest achievements are at home where he is married to Minster J. Lynnette Gregory, with whom he has six beautiful children and a fantastic grandson.